ADVANCE

C000232011

Published by
LID Publishing Limited
The Record Hall, Studio 304,
16-16a Baldwins Gardens,
London EC1N 7RJ, UK

info@lidpublishing.com
www.lidpublishing.com

A member of:

businesspublishersroundtable.com

© Jim N. R. Dale, 2020
© LID Publishing Limited, 2020

Printed by Gutenberg Press, Malta
ISBN: 978-1-912555-66-6

Cover and Page design: Caroline Li

JIM N. R. DALE

WEATHER OR NOT?

THE PERSONAL AND COMMERCIAL IMPACTS OF WEATHER AND CLIMATE

MADRID | MEXICO CITY | LONDON
NEW YORK | BUENOS AIRES
BOGOTA | SHANGHAI | NEW DELHI

CONTENTS

For every drop of rain, for every flake of snow,

For every rise and fall in the mercury,

For every breath of wind, for every ray of sunshine,

For every storm and for every halcyon day;

There is a commensurate and measurable impact upon everything and everyone.

Understand, act and prosper; or do nothing and fade to grey.

PREFACE

And so, it begins!

Weather, or more specifically weather impact, is arguably the most fundamental external factor for every living thing on this fantast planet of ours. Yet, and for the human contingent only, this all-consuming phenomenon – which governs our health, our moods, our livelihoods, our pastimes, our fortunes and all of our futures – is more often than not taken for granted, ignored or even used as an excuse for failure and defeat.

Weather is something that happens all around us, every second of every single day of our lives. It's untouchable, sometimes unfathomable, and despite various rather feeble efforts, incontrovertibly uncontrollable.

Depending upon which of its many faces it cares to show, we love it and we hate it in equal measure. We can't stop talking about it, yet when we do it's often to berate it for the hurt it brings, or simply as an easy excuse to strike up a conversation. But it is so much more than that.

1

I would like to take you on a journey of exploration and discovery, into things you may know and things you may not know about weather and its older and longer-lived peer, climate. However, this is not an anorak's book about the science of meteorology, akin to pastime books about butterflies, stamp collecting or railway engines. On the contrary, it's far from it.

The adventure I plan to take you on will delve deep into the heart and soul of weather and global climate impact, ranging across pivotal, everyday stuff, successes and failures, opportunities and threats, tales and myths, life itself, and death that comes to all.

I will share with you my experiences and encourage you to relive some of your own, dipping into our dreams and nightmares, our fears and hopes. After all, every time we wake from our sleep we are at the mercy of the elements. We're hostages to the whims of the weather and climate, as it influences what we eat and drink, the clothes we might wear and whether we're able to raise a smile or be smothered in misery.

My aim is to provide you with unique insight into the huge range of commercial and personal consequences of our ever-changing weather and climate … at a basic human level, within all aspects of our daily lives. In doing so I hope to inform, prompt and suggest, ultimately offering advice on how to maximize weather-related gains and minimize potential losses, while helping you embrace all forms of weather. Along the way, you may be surprised to find that these insights can actually change your life.

So, how might I do that while keeping you entertained and engaged?

This is not a novel, but it could easily be one. Indeed, it all starts with a short background story about me, because I want you to feel confident and comfortable enough to allow me to be your guide and your companion.

In the first chapter, **Me, Myself and I**, I will attempt to explain how in my earliest years I became enthused with – and downright and intoxicated by – the subject. Once gripped, I could not let go; once drunk, I had no option but to sober up and educate myself. It took me several decades to do so but, like any reformed drunkard, in the end I had a story to tell and valuable information to offer to anyone who might want to listen.

Of course, weather and climate aren't solely the property of the modern era. As on every inhabited planet in the Solar System and beyond, ever since the Earth was formed 4.5 billion years ago, weather and longer-term climate cycles have shaped its surface and sculpted every species that's roamed upon it.

Therefore, to appreciate the present and perhaps even begin to think about the shapes, colours and dimensions of the future, it's necessary to take a step back, to around 12,000 years ago, at the end of last ice age. In the second chapter, **Primitive Thoughts**, following a quick look back at the Earth's climate since the outset, I will don animal skins, grow a big, bushy beard and wander across frozen wastes.

From hunters and gatherers came growers and farmers, and in the aptly titled third chapter, **Make Hay While the Sun Shines**, I will venture into the world of the Great Plains – and some smaller ones, too – stepping into one of the most weather-prone vocations there is, namely farming and agriculture. Along the way we'll throw in a bit of fishing, for good measure. Yep, if you want to know about weather impact, just ask a farmer, a grower or a fisherman, all of whom were amateur meteorologists long before there were any professionals.

By now you may have a sense of how this book will unfold, moving or even leaping from one weather-impacted field, profession or everyday situation to another. You might prefer only to read those parts that directly relate to you, but the fourth chapter, **An Ill Wind, or a Breath of Fresh Air?**, is for everyone. Our very existence, and our health and wellbeing, are to a great extent weather dependent, and this chapter will explore that link and suggest how the weather impacts our mental and physical health.

The three chapters that follow will also appeal to many on both a personal and a professional level.

Eat the Sun and Drink the Rain, **Wrong Weather, Crap Clothing and Rubbish Retailers** and **Snowed Under or Rained Out?** focus upon the world of retail. We are what we eat, what we wear and what we purchase. Virtually each and every choice we make in our lives has a retail implication. For those of you who might work within the retail environment, weather's impact is massive, but it should never be used as an easy excuse for poor sales, as it so often is. I have some ideas that retailers may want to consider.

Closely allied to the world of retail are, of course, the advertising and marketing industries. In the eighth chapter, **Feel the Pulse and Press the Button**, I want to impress upon you how pivotal weather can be in the psyche of purchasing. This powerful weapon is underestimated and grossly underplayed, for reasons I will explain. For anyone attempting to promote weather-sensitive goods or services, which account for roughly 70% of everything that's bought and sold around the globe, capturing the appropriate weather moment and knowing when to let go is an art that takes appreciation and a degree of learning. In my humble experience, most marketers fail miserably in this department by taking their eye off the ball.

Meanwhile, it was US President Bill Clinton's chief political strategist, James Carville, who coined the phrase, 'It's the Economy, Stupid.' Well, if I may be so bold as to turn another phrase, **'It's the Weather, Stupid.'** And that gives us chapter nine, on the weather's impact upon the world's economies. After all – and ignoring historical empires and modern-day desert oil fortunes – weather and climate are arguably the be-all and end-all when it comes to sorting the economic powerhouses from the economic powder puffs.

And now, on to one of my favourite weather-prone vocations: sport. If you've ever stood on the terraces, or even sat in a comfortable leather seat, at a sporting event, you can't have failed to notice the weather around you, and how it made you feel, whether hot, cold, wet, windy, sunny or snowy. The bottom line here, as covered in the tenth of the chapters, **The *Real* 12th Man**, is that if the weather impacted your own thoughts and comfort, think of how it affected the players, and subsequently the outcome of the match itself.

It doesn't matter what the sport – cricket, football/soccer, American football, tennis, baseball, rugby, track and field, motor racing, horse racing, golf and the rest – weather impact is part of every sports equation. Why? Because fine margins often make the difference between winning and losing. Understanding and implementing strategies for all types of weather will definitely pay off.

When it comes to sports and the science of winning, the betting industry is inextricably linked to every nuance of every sport, even down to betting on whether or not it will snow on Christmas Day in your part of town. As silly as it sounds, people betting on this is what has given my company, British Weather Services (BWS), its longevity, which I am eternally grateful for, despite several snowflake-counting Christmases! In the eleventh chapter, **Place your Bets (Wisely)**, I'll attempt to explain how bookmakers and sportsbook providers keep their financial books onside when the weather might be offside. I'll also explore ways and means by which those who might like a little flutter can gain an edge over other punters and bookmakers alike.

Chapter twelve, **Chasing the Rainbow**, concerns itself with our leisure time – what we do, why we do it and where we do it. Weather and climate are massive factors here, governing most of the moves we might make. Meanwhile, those who work in the leisure industry are all too aware of how fortunes are made or lost on the turn of a particular weather card. Much as with retailing, there's plenty to learn and do in the leisure-time space as the weather ebbs and flows.

You can probably guess where I go with "**I'm Singing in the Rain**," chapter thirteen. The film industry, and the arts more generally, can't escape the weather's grip; indeed, it's instrumental in so many ways. Weather has been the subject of or the background wallpaper for literally thousands of songs, poems, paintings, TV shows and films, and there's a simple reason why. Our many weather types evoke emotions and passions; they provide colour and depth, atmosphere and feeling. Weather can paint a blank canvas, make a warm cinema feel distinctly chilly, and give power and tactility to a song or a poem. Lights, camera, action!

We've all been there: whether by foot, car, train, boat or plane, our journeys have at times been curtailed or delayed by one kind of weather or another. Galling, for sure! Transport and adverse weather are longtime foes, dating back to those primitive times when hunting in a raging blizzard may have been considered a handicap, as would space travel when high winds blow a rocket launch. In the fourteenth chapter, **There and Back Again**, I'll examine this all and suggest ways we can more safely and effectively move from A to B.

When the storm hits the fan, it's the job of loss adjusters to pick up the pieces and insurers' job to pay out what's covered and due. I've spent the best part of 30 years assisting in these areas, and in the chapter fifteen, **After the Storm**, I'll take you through the good, the bad and the ugly of weather-related claims, while offering some thoughts on how to mitigate potential losses.

Solicitors, lawyers, barristers and judges ... pay attention! Arguably one of the more interesting and thought-provoking areas of weather's impact involves you, and indeed anyone who has delved into the world of weather-related litigation. In the sixteenth chapter, **Every Cloud has a Legal Lining**, I'll take you through a somewhat darkened legal door and reveal things that might surprise or even shock you.

The Heat is On (or Off), chapter seventeen, concerns itself with the energy sector, where I'll offer some useful tips on how to reduce costs, and physically and financially survive heatwaves and big freezes.

In chapter eighteen, **Ready, Aim, Fire!**, I look at how weather has been a key player in virtually all wars and many, many battles since humankind first picked up a club and decided to use it against other humans. From the Battle of the Bulge and the Battle of Stalingrad to the Falklands/Malvinas war, from the First Punic War to the Iraq wars, weather has been a friend or a foe to a long line of generals and admirals. Some of them didn't realize the difference, or simply didn't bother, often with devastating results.

In chapter nineteen, **Education! Education! Education!**, I'll set out what I think we all should be learning and debating when it comes to weather and climate, for the good of individuals, companies, organizations and the planet. I'm going to suggest a big change, simply because past and present curricula, in my view, fall well short of what is useful and what is required. Please feel free to join the class.

If meaningful education is a worthwhile pursuit, then understanding and heeding weather-related warnings is definitely another. There are far more fatalities, injuries and hardships tied to severe weather events than there ever need be. In chapter twenty, **Be Warned, Be Safe!**, I'll suggest various proactive ways you can protect yourself and your family, friends and colleagues from potentially hazardous weather.

And finally, in the closing chapter, **Climate Changed**, we'll look at where we were, where we are, where we're going ... and ponder whether mankind will survive future climate changes. I won't duck and dive or push self-interest; too many politicians and others do that already. You may not like what I say, and it may even scare the pants off you, but the only way to prevent, or at least limit, a human catastrophe is to be blunt. Thankfully, being from the North of England, bluntness comes relatively easy to me!

OK, time to put on your backpack. Let's go find a comfortable, fluffy cloud to transport us on our long journey.

Just one more thing before we set off: wherever weather is concerned, remember that it will always be far more beneficial to look up at the sky than down at your feet!

CHAPTER **1**

ME, MYSELF AND I:
A SELF-MADE METEOROLOGIST

I am a self-made meteorologist. Yes, that's a bold state-ment. Indeed, it's one that requires a solid explanation, as with anyone who puts themselves forward as a so-called 'expert' in a particular field. All the more so in a field that is so obviously all-consuming to us all, or at least should be.

In these times, when experts of all shapes and colours are being trashed by politicians – particularly the populist politicians, if only because scientific facts can inconven-iently get in the way of certain political agendas – being an expert can be a dangerous and unforgiving label.

Still, I write this book and offer my advice as someone with deep knowledge and long experience in dealing with weather impacts of all kinds, including the grand-daddy of them all: climate change. If that rubs up against certain political views, alternative stances, or simply resistance to adapt or change, then I am content to be a small part of the ongoing debate, with the hope of melt-ing a few frozen minds along the way.

I was born in Manchester, England, in December 1960. Although clouded by the loss of my dad at a very young age, my earliest memories of the weather were of the cold, grey and distinctly nasty variety. By that I mean smog. We were in the latter years of 'King Coal,' with cotton mills, industrial factories and countless domestic fires belching out soot and ash like some kind of crazy, unforgiving volcano.

During high-pressure winter days with little or no wind, hands or scarves covering mouths and noses did little to prevent the poisonous infusion, and it wasn't uncommon to arrive home with an irritatingly itchy throat and a nose full of horrible black stuff.

Worse still, along with the smog, real fear was hanging in the air. Although the UK's Clean Air Act had been in force since 1956, due mainly to mass deaths in London, someone forgot to mention it to the weather gods. People were still dying by the thousands of various respiratory diseases, and even in my earliest formative years (thanks mainly to the awareness and protective nature of my mum), we tended to avoid venturing out too far, for too long, in such dreadful conditions. Instead, we were content to stay in, warm and cosy, laid out by the open coal fire. (Well, better the devil you know!)

However, not all of my early weather experiences were doom and gloom. When we look back, we tend to recall the most extreme of experiences. And during the summer of 1976, as a young teenager, I experienced a heatwave and drought of unprecedented British severity that sits long in the memory. After endless days of oppressive temperatures and dwindling reservoirs, a Minister of Drought was appointed by the UK government, instructed to help preserve water and survive the heat. It was a super rare event, and it literally governed people's moods and actions from dawn to dusk. The black tarmac streets were baking, and my mind was boiling over with respect for Mother Nature and how she could command us in our every move.

The other early memory I have of weather's magnificent influence was when I sat at home, staring out through a huge bay window, as one of the big beasts of weather, a stupendous thunderstorm, unleashed its fury. I can't easily relate what it meant to observe this thunderstorm revealing its glory in front of my eyes, but feelings of awe, excitement and fear were palpable, almost as if I had a natural affinity to the frightening majesty of lightning and thunder. It was a somewhat scary experience, but it was also awesomely beautiful. The event permeated my bones.

That feeling of being one with the weather was gradually to expand within me. To literally feel the wind in my hair, or the rain on my face, gave me a comforting feeling – almost as if I was shaking hands or hugging each of the weather's elements in turn, no matter the severity. The nearest feeling I can relate to you that might make sense is that sensation one gets when snow falls for the first time at the beginning of winter. It creates a lovely, feel-good tingle; it's something special, something mystical, something magical.

For those of you who've watched or read *The Lord of the Rings* trilogy, or even more recently HBO's *Game of Thrones* series, weather was integral in creating a depth of atmosphere and feeling. In both, the gradually deteriorating weather gave an acute sense that malicious 'others' were controlling it, culminating in a growing sense of harshness and doom. If you know what I'm talking about, I'm sure you too are more than capable of feeling the invasiveness of weather within your own bones.

Back in the late 1970s, I took a step that was to ensure that I'd meet the full force of all kinds of weather. Now, I'll be totally honest and say that, for one reason or another, I left school with qualifications that were comparable to a field of rotten turnips. Thankfully, among those useless turnips were a couple of gem lettuces. I had done well enough in the subjects of English and Geography to enable me to qualify for the British Royal Navy ... as a caterer.

The catering wasn't to last. I was OK at it, but it wasn't in my bones because something else was. And then I saw an opportunity that I'd been blind to. The Navy had a helicopter contingent, which goes under the umbrella name of The Fleet Air Arm. After a successful written test, and an equally successful interview with some tall guy with lots of gold stripes and a bunch of medals, I was accepted into the school of oceanography and meteorology.

Over the course of a year I learned everything necessary to expertly observe, assess and relay details on the weather to flight crews, including international codes for over a hundred types of conditions and thirty different cloud types. There was a final examination to pass, which to this day I see as the equivalent to a degree, but for me it was a simple task. After all, weather was in my bones and all I had to do was bleed.

So, off I went, sailing the seven seas (well, five of them). But I was being paid for staring up at the heavens and out at the deep blue oceans, doing what came very naturally. Surely, it couldn't get much better than this ... but it did!

When I was a young 20-something, the Falklands War (or, if you prefer, the Battle for the Malvinas) started. For most of the conflict, I was stationed in an underground bunker near London, plotting and drawing South Atlantic weather charts, as weather and war are inextricably linked. (This is something I'll cover in greater detail later in this book).

Then, I got a chance to head south on what amounted to an ex-colonial liner, the SS Uganda. It was a truly surreal few weeks, travelling through the tropics on a rich man's pleasure cruiser, heading for the aftermath of war on an island at the bottom of the world. (Yes, luckily for me, the war had ended before I arrived). But it was my experiences in and around the Falklands – and also the tiny, utterly captivating island of South Georgia – that were to stick with me to this day.

Both island groups, and the thousand miles of ferocious ocean in-between, are a meteorological observer's fantasy come true. That part of the world is raw and unforgiving; humankind is wholly insignificant. Everything happens with speed and ferocity, often with little or no warning. Tempestuous, never-ending seas, hurricane-force winds, hidden icebergs and snarling glaciers make skilled weather-watchers worth their weight in sunken gold.

I spent six unforgettable months in those breathtaking zones, sucking up all the weather impact I could handle, along with ultra-breathable air that was extraordinary clear and pure. I was proud to be able to prompt captains and commanders to change course in order to avoid potential disaster, and proud not to have to use an anti-aircraft killing weapon that the powers that be had put me in charge of. I was no longer a lucky boy with a hobby for a job, I was a young man with purpose, passion and more worldly experience than I could have ever imagined.

However, for reasons I still somewhat regret, it wasn't too many years before I decided to leave the Navy and embark upon a civilian life close to London. For two years I dallied with odd jobs in and around the bustling urban 'centre of the universe,' a little like a wandering albatross in those endless concrete seas, sometimes lost, sometimes confused, often wishing I was back in my safe meteorological world of the South Atlantic.

And then, as it does, the sun rose again.

A marine company based in the City of London made contact with me, seeking a meteorologist to assist with their expanding ventures. In the UK at that time, only the government's Meteorological Office provided weather information to the masses, so there was a real opportunity for this company to rise up and compete. I was there for two years, but to cut a long story short, they booted the ball over the top of the highest and widest commercial open goal that ever existed. Redundancies followed, and I was to be one of a small handful to be shown the open door.

I stress the word *open* because after receiving the fateful redundancy notice via a telephone call to my newly acquired and heavily mortgaged home, I walked through another more magnificent open door that was to change my life forever. In October 1987, just after the 'Great Storm,' which devastated southern parts of the UK, from the ashes and debris that surrounded me I founded the private company British Weather Services (BWS). The Meteorological Office frowned, just a bit.

It was still the time of typewriters and Amstrad green-screen computers – with the internet still being formed in the very clever mind of a fellow Brit, Tim Berners-Lee – so things mostly happened via landline telephones and those mysteriously amazing facsimile machines. There was no social media and no pretty weather icons, care of Google or anybody else. This was hands-on and a bloody hard slog at times. But that would turn out to be a blessing.

I was proficient enough at communicating, and even better at seeing commercial opportunities. One could also say that I was outspoken, and that front-footed attitude had partly led to my London redundancy (treading on toes and all that). But what I saw revolved around supplying one- to seven-day regional weather outlooks for the UK via a premium-rate telephone service line, to be equally shared with the still frowning Meteorological Office.

Within one month of launch, I received a cheque for more than double what I was earning in a year in my former London post. Houston, we had liftoff!

Over the next thirty-odd years, the world changed dramatically. Weather interpretation and dissemination changed, markedly. The British and world economies changed and changed again. And, most alarmingly, the global climate also changed. All of that and more were hurdles that required leaping if BWS and I were going to survive into the future, as other purveyors of weather information came and went. To prosper was going to require imagination, innovation and perseverance.

In the chapters to come, I hope you will gain insight into how we did that, and into the weather-sensitive sectors my colleagues and I worked in. The scope and diversity were, and still are, staggering, and at times surprising and even shocking.

I believe I can convey to you some useful information, even if I end up posing more questions than I give answers. Are you still holding tight to our cloud?

CHAPTER 2

PRIMITIVE THOUGHTS: THOUGHTS: CLIMATE RULES - EVOLVE OR DIE!

Earth, 4.5 billion years ago: newborn and seeking a destiny, following the planetary collision known as the Theia Impact, which many geoscientists also believe formed our Moon.

Molten and likely void of oxygen, our planet was an angry tempest. This wasn't weather or climate; it was the boiling blood of a planetary car crash, coupled with further bombardments from space caused by the shifting orbits of nearby planets. Things were destined to settle down, and they did, though painfully slowly in the grand scale of time.

Life – but definitely not as we know it – is believed to have gained an initial foothold some 4 billion years ago within the newly formed oceans. For that to happen, even in the most simplistic, inorganic molecular form, meant the Earth had evolved enough to support that most basic of life. Yet, oxygen and photosynthesis were not yet part of the equation. Nitrogen, methane, carbon dioxide and other greenhouse gases ruled. If there was a climate, it was a rudimentary one, but one that contained rain and was ever-changing and evolving.

Over the next couple billion years, other ultra-primitive life forms came and went. Around 1.7 billion years ago, multicellular organisms arrived on the scene, aided by a steady increase of oxygen in the atmosphere. Sea-borne algae, followed by land plants, came into the picture between 1 billon and 800 million years ago, further increasing the oxygen count.

The most recent 550 million years of Earth's history saw the birth of the arthropods, flowers, dinosaurs, birds, primates, and finally – right at the pointy end of the time spectrum – came humankind. Day-to-day weather and longer-term climate were by now key to the very existence of a huge diversity of living things. But there was an inherent snag: climate was forever on the move.

There are various reasons why climate has changed over many millennia. The main one is the amount of sunlight reaching the land masses of the northern hemisphere due to Earth's proximity to the Sun, and the changing angle of our planet's axis to the Sun. Other reasons include carbon dioxide fluctuations within the oceans and the atmosphere, tectonic plate movements and volcanic activity, meteorite impacts, changes in the flow of ocean currents, and last but not least man-made climate change.

Over the 444 million years since the first mass extinction, climate change has been a life giver and a life taker in almost equal measures. Of the five great mass extinctions within that period, at least three were directly or indirectly caused by climate change, including the biggest one. At the end of the Permian Age, 251 million years ago, some 96% of living things perished as the climate cried tears of poison under an ultra-toxic mixture of carbon dioxide, methane and hydrogen sulphide.

Of course, we humans had nothing to do with it; we were but a tiny twinkle in somebody's (or something's) eye.

This extinction was a result of a deadly cocktail of natural catastrophes, but it was and still is a stark warning written in the DNA of the Earth's soul to all those that might wish to inhabit this blue and green planet. That warning: 'Climate rules – evolve or die!'

And then, for the future good of mammals, including mankind, following a highly successful reign of some 250 million years, dinosaurs fell from the Earth. (Or, rather, they fell into it.) Sixty-six million years ago, the climate lurched again, following what appeared to have been the twin wallops of a massive asteroid impact in Mexico's Yucatan Peninsula and super-volcanic activity across west-central India.

While some 75% of life on Earth perished or failed to evolve following these cataclysms, one thing evolved quite nicely indeed, and it had hair.

It's only in the last 200,000 years or so, a tiny microcosm of the Earth's existence, that we humans have picked up the mantle as the so-called superior species and, of late, the self-proclaimed guardians of the planet. Within that period, global climate and climate zones have fluctuated wildly, just as the weather through the seasons has ebbed and flowed. Ice ages and warm interglacial periods have come and gone, and great civilizations have been lost to heat, cold, flood and drought.

And yet, even with the rising profile of global climate change and occasional catastrophic weather events,

I suspect that the majority of us in our fast-paced world are largely ambivalent, or at best only reactive, to weather or climate effects. We certainly don't seem all that proactive in the face of various climatic twists and turns.

Dare I say it, most in the developed world (and I even include myself on occasion) take the weather for granted, largely cocooned off from the nasty stuff and insensitive to and disinterested in everyday, run-of the-mill conditions. We have far too many modern-day distractions to think too deeply about the weather, unless it happens to be extreme. But it wasn't always like that.

I promised in this chapter to take you on a journey back to around 12,000 years ago, to get a feel for how weather might have played a part in primitive culture. Around a thousand years prior to that, it's thought that a comet had crashed into the Earth and had brought about sudden, dramatic global cooling. A mini-ice age was the result, and since we're making this journey together, I guess we had better get ourselves suitably dressed for the occasion!

So here we are, somewhere in mid-central France (near modern Dijon), in deepest, darkest December, looking out on members of the Stone Age Magdalenian tribe. No passports or visas are required ... perhaps just a few handy spears and clubs. There are about three hundred individuals in all, living within a large, shallow cave system.

Bright fires flicker within the caves and family groups crowd around the flames, striving to soak up the glorious warmth. They have to, for temperatures outside have not risen above freezing for the past fortnight and overnight temperatures have been truly deadly. Across the plain and within the surrounding pine forest, crusty snow lies several inches deep, and a bitter glacial wind blows in from the empty icelands to the east. The word 'harsh' does not do justice to these cruel and unforgiving conditions.

But the Magdalenians are tough and resilient; they also have much more body hair than we do today, which can be useful in such a harsh climate. As a culture they have been in existence for several thousand years, through many unforgiving winters and unproductive summers.

This particular group have done well. In the previous lukewarm summer, they managed to grow or gather an assortment of crops, roots, berries, mushrooms and tubers. A newly invented harpoon also helped them harvest a bountiful supply of salmon and trout. Best of all, stacked or hung in a large cave larder and half a dozen animal skin-sheathed wooden huts were the slain bodies of antelopes, reindeer, bison, horses and rabbits. There was even a juvenile woolly mammoth, frozen solid and splayed out in the open air, awaiting a springtime barbeque. (Although scientists differ on this point, the sad likelihood is that primitive man, and not climate change, finally killed off the mammoths.)

This Magdalenian tribe, like every other prehistoric clan at the time, lived and breathed the weather from dawn until dusk. They had no religion as such, and few if any diversions. Weather was their hope and their salvation. In one of the caves, zodiacal paintings are evident, signifying the paths of the sun, the moon and certain planets. There are also images of their crops, the animals that wandered the forests and plains, their hunting weapons, simple jewellery and other important icons of this time.

They paint how they live; they depict what is most important to them. The life-giving sun, pagan-like god or not, is their *Mona Lisa*, *The Last Supper* and *The Starry Night*, all rolled into one.

I could go on to paint my own story of this resourceful Magdalenian tribe, and how they may have succumbed to the big freeze, or indeed lived through that particular grim winter, feasting on mammoth steaks and succulent salmon in the relative warmth of the spring that followed. It may have well happened like that – after all, they were all too aware that the weather was their everything, and they were far better than we ever could be at reading nature's daily signals. However, weather was also their nemesis, and they knew that too, as did others that came before and after them.

Since mankind first walked the Earth, countless civilizations have survived or perished at the hands of a changing climate or individual severe weather events. The warnings are literally written in stone, usually long abandoned.

Some 400 years ago, drought – and not just an odd dry year, but several hundred years of minimal rainfall – put pay to the Akkadian Empire of Mesopotamia (today's northeast Syria/southeast Turkey). The same fate befell the Mayans in Mesoamerica (Central America), between the 8th and 9th centuries. A devastating drought followed by a violent monsoon wiped out the fierce Khymer (Angkor) empire of Southeast Asia in the latter part of the 15th century. Around the same time, give or take a few hundred years, the mighty Vikings of Scandinavia were forced to flee their settlements in Greenland as what is known as 'The Little Ice Age' took hold and made human life virtually impossible.

Climate change, we've seen again and again through history, can provide for life, but it can also be a savage executioner.

On this occasion, however, let's quietly leave the scene and allow our courageous Magdalenian tribe to live long and prosper through their long dark winter and into a spring of hope and opportunity. Meanwhile ... can someone pass the Dijon mustard?

CHAPTER **3**

MAKE HAY WHILE THE SUN SHINES: FARMING, AGRICULTURE AND FISHING

If you are looking for the most pivotal and important relationship between climate, weather and our past and present as humans, then you've found it here.

The following are some candid comments by Peter King, a dyed-in-the-wool northern English farmer, agronomist and contractor, and also a user of BWS's services for many a year:

"The weather is singularly the most important element that affects farm production. It affects crop growth, yield and health, and for that matter any sort of farm activity carried out during the growing season. I, like my father and grandfather before me, farm in the northwest of the UK, in the wetter grassland country.

"My granddad's lifestyle was beautifully simple; he farmed in sympathy with the seasons. But even as a child I understood that our harvest, and that meant haymaking, took priority over all farm tasks until it was completed. Securing the farm's winter feed was of paramount importance. A poor hay crop meant a winter of meager returns, ill-thriven cattle and the danger of contracting farmer's lung.

"We can't fight the weather, and, even today, with my monster machines that can carry out more work in an hour than granddad could do in twenty-four, a spell of inclement weather at the wrong time brings me to my knees. The weather makes it impossible to farm as granddad once did.

"We have to work under the open sky, and we are greatly reliant upon the weather – we have no choice but to suffer its moody conditions. So, when you next return to work, whether it's in an office or factory, imagine doing your job without a roof over your head."

I guess that says an awful lot!

Whether growing naturally, farmed or out of the ocean, humans and indeed all living things could never have existed if it were not for the integral relationship between Mother Nature's natural larder and the weather. That contingency of course applies across the spectrum of wildlife, livestock, crops and natural vegetation, including the very first microorganisms.

An appropriate temperature range, the precise mixture of various atmospheric gases and our precious H2O have made for the delightful blue, green and white pigments of Planet Earth all those jealous aliens see from space. The brown and orange smudges are where it hasn't quite worked out, where most life has for the most part paused, or indeed where it's gone badly wrong.

Now, I'm a professional meteorologist in one guise or another, but of all those from other vocations I've met or conversed through the years, it's the farmers, growers, agriculturists and fishermen that come closest to pinching my clothes. By that, and taking Peter King as a prime example, I mean they tend to know their stuff when it comes to weather impact and indeed weather prediction, and so they should. Their livelihoods, and sometimes even their lives themselves, depend upon the vagaries of the weather coming good to nurture their crops, live-stock or the ocean's bounty, season after season, year after year. It's a little like a gambler placing chips on black or red and hoping the balls land in the right slots, time and time again ... which they sometimes don't.

I know of many in agriculture and fishing who not only look to public weather forecasts for guidance, but gal-lantly attempt to forecast the weather for themselves by looking at what's around them. 'Weather forecasting by nature' is an age-old pursuit and a subject of great debate. Animals, insects, birds, plants, the sky, the sea and other aspects of nature all fall into the prediction fold. Some of these are simply reacting to changes in air pressure, humidity, wind and temperature. However, these guys will tell you (and I'll back them up) that there are certain valid natural clues to prospective changes in the weather.

I thought it might be entertaining, and hopefully of some use, to list a number of historical sayings, signs and prov-erbs that have been linked to changes in the weather, in order to gauge their usefulness and validity. Let's call it an exercise in separating the wheat from the chaff, or indeed the fish from the plastic!

Make hay while the sun shines. Of course! It's not so much about what is about to arrive, but making the most of the sunshine that's already in place. Hay making doesn't work very well in the damp or wet, but copious sunshine allows for the hay to be more easily cut, dried and bundled. But this saying is much more than about hay making; it's about working in *any* vocation in the most favourable conditions. In my own words, 'Feel the pulse and capture the moment,' which applies across the board, in every type of weather. Validity verdict: 10/10.

Cows sitting in a field means rain is imminent. Really? Pull the other udder. Cows sitting or lying usually means they're resting or chewing the cud. Sure, cattle like their comfort as much as every other beast of the field, but there is no scientific evidence that they plonk themselves down on a nice dry patch ahead of rain. They do, on the other hand, seek shelter from inclement weather once it's arrived, which can be to their acute detriment when sheltering under trees during a thunderstorm. Validity verdict: 1/10.

Early rodent infestation indicates a tough winter to come. This adage stems from some farmers' belief that an invasion of rats, mice and other vermin into the farm holdings during late autumn means an unusually cold winter to follow, as some mammals and birds are uniquely sensitive to minute, but ultimately significant, longer-term weather changes. Well, it's either that or maybe there's more available grub in the warm inside than the cold outdoors! However, I do not entirely dismiss certain animals' talent for predicting the weather, as it's critical to them and almost certainly in their bones. Validity verdict: 6/10.

If flowers smell more strongly than usual, then rain is on the way. Although I'm happy to stand corrected on this one, I feel this is about rising humidity. More often than not, when humidity levels rise, rain is indeed approaching. Many plants bask, and engage in their most promiscuous behaviour, in the rain, and you don't go very far in this life (unless you happen to be a skunk) without smelling nice. Validity verdict: 8/10.

To convert cricket chirps to degrees Fahrenheit, count the number of chirps over 14 seconds then add 40 to get the temperature. You know what, I can't really be bothered! OK, I accept that their chirp rate may increase or decrease at the peaks or troughs of temperature, but to suggest crickets are the next greatest thermometer is a chirp too far. Entomologists, prove me wrong! Validity verdict: 4/10.

If it rains before seven, it will be clear before eleven. This one isn't so much about the time of day, but more to do with the average time it takes a frontal rain system to pass – generally three hours. As a rule of thumb, I can buy this one, though it obviously comes a cropper with quasi-stationary (slow moving or waving) fronts. But for the most part, you can count on an hour either side of the three-hour marker. Validity verdict: 7/10.

There you go, a few of the many good, bad and down-right silly tenets of self-forecasting the weather.

The fact is, modern-day, professional forecasting techniques have long since overridden amateur efforts. Indeed, of all the forecast enquiries we've received here at BWS, well over 80% have come from farmers and, of those, half originate from the lush green and temperate lands of the Republic of Ireland. Is it that they don't trust their own public weather broadcaster? Or, is there a strong desire to chew the cud in person, with frank and earnest northern English types?

To be honest, it goes back to the weather being the true be-all and end-all for them – the judge and jury, deciding whether they can pay the bills and feed the family with a little more than potatoes, turnips or sprats at the end of a long, hard season. Talking things through with a trusted forecaster when it comes to pivotal decisions regarding silaging, haymaking, harvesting, safe fishing and looking after their livestock is to them an absolute necessity.

Pretty weather icons on a smartphone don't quite provide the necessary confidence, and most are wise enough to recognize that they need more. They need a 'guardian' to help them be as sure as they can possibly be ... or at worst, someone to blame when it all goes wrong!

Now, I'm not going to end this particular chapter without mentioning man-made climate change, because intensive farming methods have been, and continue to be, one of the main contributors to global warming. Human sustenance may well start in the vast fields of farmed land and fished oceans, but the vast majority of land use has been at the expense of trees and natural plants that have soaked up carbon dioxide for thousands of years. Add biodiversity losses, accelerated soil erosion, machine-intensive fishing and farming, pollution, acidification and plastification of our rivers and oceans – not to mention the gas emissions of billions of livestock – and, *hey presto*, we've created a problem!

To give you an idea the scale of that problem, let's take one farm animal as an example. Cattle living their lives in the developed western world emit some 110–130 kg of methane gas per animal, per year. That's compared to 0.10–0.14 kg for the average human. Given that methane is approximately 30 times more potent a greenhouse gas than CO_2, do you begin to appreciate what I mean by ongoing causal effects?

We all have to eat, of course, and somebody has to provide for that, so let's not simply pile the blame for climate ills solely on farmers and growers. Still, it's still interesting to note the carbon footprint of a few of the everyday items we might consume.

My thanks to Jane Richards of Greeneatz.com for providing some very digestible figures, including the equivalent car miles driven to release the same climate-changing emissions per 1 kilo of the named food item.

Rank	Food	CO_2 Kilos Equivalent	Car Miles Equivalent
1	Lamb	39.2	91
2	Beef	27.0	63
3	Cheese	13.5	31
4	Pork	12.1	28
5	Turkey	10.9	25
6	Chicken	6.9	16
7	Tuna	6.1	14
8	Eggs	4.8	11
9	Potatoes	2.9	7
10	Rice	2.7	6
11	Nuts	2.3	5
12	Beans/Tofu	2.0	4.5
13	Vegetables	2.0	4.5
14	Milk	1.9	4
15	Fruit	1.1	2.5
16	Lentils	0.9	2

To be totally honest, I like my protein-providing turkey, and I'm partial to a piece of feta cheese and a daily egg. But I'm also pleased to say that in recent years my own diet has shifted far more toward those items occupying the bottom of the list, though I've still got to get to grips with the delights of tofu.

I'll return to man-made climate change with a vengeance in the final chapter, but I'd like to say here and now that my beef (pardon the pun) concerning the causes of climate change does not lie with the majority of good and honest farmers and growers, and neither should yours. Yes, there are baddies – the unbridled polluters and the 'couldn't give a damn' types – but you'll find ignorant individuals in every industry.

So, to round things off, please allow me to breathe deeply and say the following to the farmers, growers, agriculturists and fishermen of the world:

First, be agile as you move into the future. Diversify where possible, and head in a direction of sustainable practices that favour protecting the Earth and reducing your climate footprint. When you can afford it, move into using battery-powered robots to replace diesel tractors, and drones and sensors to provide more accurate and targeted use of pesticides, herbicides and fertilizers. Plant more trees for more reasons than you think, and select animals that produce less methane. Try to engage with political and fashion changes, and anticipate demand (what's likely to go out of fashion and what's likely to replace it).

Meanwhile, if a spokesperson or politician says to you that man-made climate change is 'fake news,' they aren't doing you and your family, friends or industry any favours. Such individuals ignore the indisputable scientific facts and have but one aim, which is to consider themselves over everybody and everything else. More often than not, they snuggle up to those profiteering companies at the forefront of polluting the atmosphere and the oceans.

In this arena of intensive weather and climate impact, I'm only too ready to help separate the wholesome wheat from the political chaff. Why do I bother mentioning any of this? The answer is simple: the Earth as we know it is dying, but the inhabitants wish to survive ... and they need to eat.

CHAPTER **4**

AN ILL WIND, OR A BREATH OF FRESH AIR?:
HEALTH AND WELLBEING

I want you to do something for me. Well, it's for you, really.

When you wake up in the morning, and just before you draw back the curtains, give yourself a score out of ten for how you're feeling, whatever you may be experiencing at the time. Once you've done that, let in the light (or dark) of the day, and within ten seconds score yourself again. Do that over several days, noting any differences. My guess is that your feelings of positivity, neutrality or negativity will be skewed by the prevailing weather you observe out of your window.

When I say weather, and so long as your view takes in more than merely the neighbouring brick wall, your instant reaction will be tuned in to the colour of the sky.

It's not by chance that sky blue, yellow and green are considered by behavioral scientists to be the ultimate in pleasing and calming colours. Allow me to explain why.

We have to step back a couple of chapters, to prehistoric times, to appreciate that these three colours meant life and opportunity at its most basic. Blue meant a clear sky with no hazards, yellow the splendour of life-giving sunshine, and green the burgeoning growth of healthy vegetation. Those feel-good colours were key (particularly after long hard winters) and have been passed on through the ages – the natural feel-good reaction imprinted within all of our genes. Yes, we all have the weather in our bones to one degree or another!

Ok, I know what you might be thinking: there are plenty of alternative weather conditions and associated colours that can make or change our emotional state. We do, of course, need skies of grey or near-black to bring helpful rains, and the first snows of winter carpeting the ground in crystal white tend to bring a feeling of childish joy to most. Meanwhile, the seven colours of a rainbow or a red and orange sunrise or sunset can be magical, while brilliant white lightning evokes fascination and a sense of majesty.

Nevertheless, for humans to function at our best, we require calmness and a mental feeling of inner control. And that's largely provided by those three essential, comforting pigments – blue, yellow and green.

Weather is *the* fundamental provider and taker of life – quite literally, a breath of fresh air or an ill wind. Weather will have an impact, whether it's invisible to you or quite apparent, on your everyday life, either directly or indirectly, and here's how.

Let's do the life-giving festival first. We only have to look at flora and fauna in all their forms to appreciate that the right mix of weather is the catalyst for procreation, and subsequently the survival and extension of the species. I guess there are a few exceptions out there at the back of a deep, dark cave, or at the bottom of a dark, super-pressurized ocean. But in the vast majority of cases, sexual and asexual activity is a finely tuned event, inextricably linked to certain atmospheric and oceanographic conditions such as air pressure, temperature, humidity, wind speed, rainfall, snowfall and the daddy of them all, sunshine.

The seasons are brought about by the tilt of the Earth's axis in relation to the sun, and they're the main drivers of plant, insect and animal reproduction, which go into overdrive during the spring and summer months of both hemispheres. Sexual activity will rise and fall broadly in line with the movement of the overhead sun; it's almost as if a big party light has been switched on and everything and everyone joins the soiree, seeking out a mate before the big boss with the overcoat and wooly scarf switches off the mood music.

You see, we're back to feelings, moods and mental states – all chemically-driven, often weather-influenced, and part of everyday life for every living thing. Stress caused by the 'wrong' weather, and a subsequent chemical imbalance, are the enemies of normal, cyclical reproduction, but 99% of life reacts to the appropriate party conditions, and that to some degree includes human life.

So, do we humans procreate more in the spring months of March, April and May, as the sun creeps ever higher in the sky? Hardly! Given that July, August and September are the peak birth months, it appears the sun-shy months of October, November and December are the choice times to dance the fandango. That could be for two reasons.

The first is that babies born in the warmer summer months historically stood a better chance of survival in their first few weeks, when mortality rates were at their highest. So, it was, and maybe still is (for differing global reasons) a planned-survival thing. The second factor is that in temperate, continental and polar climates, the dark and cold tend to mean longer times spent in the warmth and comfort of our beds ... and that simply means opportunity knocking. There is a third reason, which is arguably not weather related, which is the occurrence of certain festivities, including Christmas, New Year, Diwali, Hanukkah and other such celebrations, during this period.

By the way, sunlight sets off chemical reactions that naturally raise our libidos, but when it comes with excessive heat or excessive cold, forget it – our bodies are not into overheated, or frigid, workouts!

Illness and death are also a big part of the equation of life. Throughout history, and to this day, diseases that are directly or indirectly weather-related have been the cause of far more illness and death than all the wars put together. The list is lengthy and horribly impressive: influenza, cholera, typhoid, pneumonia, tuberculosis, dysentery, the plague, malaria and dengue fever all have a weather association of one kind or another. In fact, a change in the weather can help bring an end to certain catastrophic epidemics. As I pen this chapter, the coronavirus pandemic is in full swing around the globe; you will now know whether the dawn of spring and summer in the northern hemisphere has helped to reduce the impact (or not).

Meanwhile, the top present-day killer, which accounts for almost one third of all human deaths, is cardiovascular disease, followed by cancer and then respiratory diseases. Where's the weather impact in those? Well, I'm not pretending that weather-related deaths have greatly reduced as a percentage of all deaths over the past couple of centuries, but all three of the above afflictions have a significant weather association. For example, extreme heat and extreme cold do lead to a spike in heart attacks; overexposure to the sun has led to a tenfold increase in skin cancers over the past few decades; respiratory diseases caused by heat, lackluster winds and increased pollution, are a ghastly, resurgent threat.

I could go on and on, without even mentioning the hundreds of more minor weather-associated ailments that each of us endures within our lifetimes. But, I want to end this chapter with a couple of thoughts that encapsulate the relationship between weather impact and our wellbeing.

The first concerns mental health, and specifically suicide. Suicide accounts for a staggering 1.5% of all deaths annually, with some 75% of that total made up of males. It's not by chance that the world's highest suicide rates occur in countries of extreme heat or extreme cold, like Sri Lanka and Lithuania. I'm not suggesting that higher suicide levels are tied purely to weather extremes, but unrelenting heat and humidity, or depressingly cold and dark weather, surely can't help in times of acute desperation. Just think about how you might feel under endless days of insufferable weather. Although there will be other social, economic, political and hereditary reasons for suicidal tendencies, stressful weather may well be a pivotal part of the equation.

Let's go back to where I started in this chapter: clear blue skies, a brilliant golden-yellow sun and the glory of green growth, all amping up the feel-good factor. Well, gloomy, cold, sunless caves have precisely the opposite effect, and can only add to levels of depression, as can day after day of heat and high humidity. It's therefore apt to mention the condition known as seasonal affective disorder (SAD), where long, dark hours and periods of debilitating weather has a huge negative mental and physical impact upon many thousands of sufferers, with countless others impacted to a lesser degree.

I'm far from being a psychiatrist, and won't pretend that fine, temperate weather is the key to a positive state of mind. Yet, I'm convinced that exposure to those comforting colours – and production of the 'happiness' chemical serotonin, which sunshine naturally stimulates – can help create a more positive mindset. And I'm convinced that this applies not only in the most needy of cases, but for every one of us when, from time to time, we inevitably feel the world pressing down on us.

Meanwhile, natural disasters – including extreme heat and cold, wildfires, hurricanes and typhoons, tornadoes, floods, droughts and wind-driven tidal surges – account for around 1% of deaths worldwide each year. On the face of it, and particularly when such events feature regularly in the media, the figure appears pretty low when compared to deaths caused by all forms of cancer, which clock in at 17%. However, with the rapid acceleration of global warming in recent times, I can only see this percentage rising ... and rising faster than any of us would like.

Simply put, more heat in the atmosphere = more energy = greater instances of extreme weather events. I'll explain more in the final chapter, but take it from me: the survival and the wellbeing of every species is largely dependent upon the vagaries of the weather, and now, more than ever, our rapidly changing climate.

If you work in the health and wellbeing sectors, you could do far worse than to monitor, measure, appreciate and then act upon the huge and significant part weather and climate can play in our lives. There will be a weather association to many, if not most, things that go on in your local surgery or hospital. Weather and changing climate are pivotal players, and I believe we are only scratching the tip of the iceberg when it comes to the anticipation and planning of health-related impacts and preventative measures.

For everyone else, the next time you start feeling 'under the weather,' it may well be that you're literally *under the weather*. When you are not quite yourself, in whatever way, monitor and take note of both your mental and physical health in relation to the atmospheric conditions at the time. (You know those pains in your joints on a humid day?) I can't promise that you'll be able to swerve and stave off all future weather-related maladies, but you may gain some knowledge about their origins.

As they say, knowledge is power, and nothing is more powerful than your own health!

CHAPTER 5

EAT THE SUN AND DRINK THE RAIN: RETAIL, FOOD AND BEVERAGE

It's not so much that we are what we eat, it's more like we eat for how we feel. As already mentioned, the weather more often than not governs our moods and desires, and there's no bigger daily desire than to eat and drink.

I'm now going to take you back to the words I stated at the beginning of this book, because they perfectly sum up our reaction to every aspect of weather and how that might control a good deal of what we consume.

> *For every drop of rain, for every flake of snow,*
> *For every rise and fall in the mercury,*
> *For every breath of wind, for every ray of sunshine,*
> *For every storm and for every halcyon day;*
> *There is a commensurate and measurable impact*
> *upon everything and everyone.*
> *Understand, act and prosper; or do nothing and*
> *fade to grey.*

Allow me to dwell for a moment on those periods in mankind's history, and sadly even in the present day, when food and water shortages, due mainly to drought, have led to untold disaster for entire civilizations. This is the ultimate when it comes to the negative knock-on impacts of extreme weather or climate change.

When nothing grows, livestock dies, and when water sources dry up, that's when we can truly put an empty supermarket shelf into perspective. There are few if any choices for those poor souls, simply because the weather (sometimes coupled with civil war) has reduced their status to one of honourable beggars, dependent upon the goodwill of charities, NGOs and governments.

I'll pick up on this again in the final chapter, but let me now turn to some other fundamentals that likely apply to the majority of you reading this book.

Our body operates optimally at a temperature close to 36.8 degrees Celsius (98.2 degrees Fahrenheit). Any deviation, up or down, will lead us to crave certain foodstuffs or beverages. The greater the deviation, the greater the desire, and it's often not the weather that sways us one way or another. Whether it's ambient air temperature, humidity, wind, snow, direct sunshine (or the lack of it), every fluctuation drives our insatiable demand for comfort foods.

The biggest deviations accompany heatwaves and major freezes, driving major spikes in the demand for what I'm going to call the 'iceberg and volcano consumables.' If I mention water, salad, ice cream, soups, stews and pies, I'm sure you can appreciate where I'm coming from on both ends of the spectrum.

In truth, there are hundreds of such consumable items, and each in turn will have a 'melting point,' at which demand can outstrip supply. It also happens to be the point (or at least the point just prior to) where suppliers and retailers can make the greatest profit, if they're so inclined. After all, it's a boiling hot and humid volcano day, you are extremely thirsty, the queue at the only supermarket in town is out the door, but a guy selling ice-cold cans of Coke for triple the normal cost suddenly appears on the corner. Are you a buyer or not? Of course you are!

Now, from time to time those 'iceberg' and 'volcano' items can be deceiving, in terms of when the 'melting point' might be reached. A couple of years ago I did some work for Unilever, the big transnational consumer goods company. At the outset, I was asked in what kind of weather the famous Ben & Jerry's ice cream tub might reach a sales peak. I, of course, expected it would be on hot, sunny, summer days. Wrong! It was in fact on warm but rainy summer days. Why? Well, it's a comfort thing; consumers buy this item to consume indoors, while watching TV or playing electronic games, when the weather outside is inhospitable.

The moral of that story is that in order to accurately gauge the demand for a consumable item, you have to compare and contrast sales under all the weather elements, and I mean ALL of them. For example, an otherwise warm and sunny day might be offset by a stiff, cold wind. Sales on a cold day, with snow on the ground, might be accompanied by light winds, a brilliantly blue sky and copious sunshine.

The bottom line, which is so often missed by suppliers and retailers, is that if you don't measure the weather's impact on the sales performance of your goods, you are literally trading blind.

That not only applies to the 'iceberg' and 'volcano' consumables; it's true for every single item that's for sale, to one degree or another. Take a simple chicken sandwich, for instance. There will be 'melting points' where an added piece of chilled lettuce or a spoonful of hot mustard will make all the difference in whether the sandwich sells, largely depending on sunshine and temperature levels. The same might apply to a particular flavour of crisps – do beef crisps sell more than prawn cocktail crisps in deepest mid-winter? I could provide an educated guess, but frankly I don't know because I've not compared the two flavours vis-à-vis the weather ... but crisp manufacturers and retailers would do well to know.

For suppliers and manufacturers with a large factory workforce, measuring weather can also mean anticipating workplace absenteeism, something that I know from experience is massively influenced by a variety of weather elements.

In short, and to quote a favourite little guideline of mine, 'Feel the pulse and capture the moment!' Sadly, there are far too many suppliers and retailers out there who don't even roll their sleeves up, let alone feel the pulse. Instead, they use detrimental weather as an excuse for poor performance.

Sometimes that's entirely valid and sometimes it's not, but don't take my word for it. Here are some sage words from Andrew Busby, founder and CEO of Retail Reflections, *Forbes* contributor, Global Top 20 Retail Influencer and IBM Futurist:

"Not a week seems to go by without the weather being blamed for poor retail sales. Not only is this lazy, in today's world it is simply unacceptable. Instead of an excuse for poor performance, the weather can and should be used for competitive advantage. Consultant meteorologists like Jim [that's me, your humble author] not only understand this, but they are absolutely essential in ensuring retailers act intelligently, positively and purposely. CEOs, please take note!"

I thank you for the vote of confidence, Andrew. It's always good to be recognized and validated by someone with such far-reaching tentacles across the retail sector.

Now, here's something for you to do as an everyday shopper. Take a walk down an aisle in a supermarket, your local grocer or the town square market. Take note of the weather (the more extreme the better) and observe what's moving off the shelves and what's not. Better still, take a good look at your own shopping basket. How much of what you grabbed will you attribute to the day's weather and how you might be feeling? You may well be surprised, but perhaps not if you're taking this all in. Shopping baskets tend to fill commensurate with all aspects of the weather of the moment, or short-term, high-impact weather forecasts, such as imminent hard-freezes or approaching hurricanes.

Meanwhile, back on the retailer side of the counter, I have some further advice. Take onboard the most reputable forecasts you can find. Don't delude yourself into thinking that Google, Alexa or the weather icon on your smartphone are the best predictors of weather events. They're often the simplest but usually not the best. All tend to utilize a single predictive forecasting model, and no model is beyond inaccuracies. A cursory, single-tap snapshot doesn't always uncover the intricate nuances within an approaching weather system.

Nowadays, monthly and seasonal forecasts are increasingly accurate, and can be very useful in longer-term planning. After all, how useful would it be to your business to know how the month ahead is likely to pan out? And yes, yes, yes, compare sales figures to weather history, because you need a map of past sales to accurately anticipate the future.

But there's another, increasingly critical action one can take. Poor weather will have an impact on footfall … and therefore on sales. That's not rocket science; it's common sense.

So, in my mind, brick-and-mortar outlets require a proactive change of gear to effectively connect with customers at differing levels. I'll explore this in more detail over the next few chapters, but for food and beverage outlets, think about offering your customers loss leaders – a little something to make them feel better as they venture out in adverse conditions, for example. It could be as simple as a free ice-lolly on a sapping hot day, or a comforting cup of hot chocolate on a miserably cold and wet one.

All it takes is a little imagination, and your customers will thank you for it.

Why bother with any of this, you may ask. It's because we *really do* eat the sunshine and drink the rain!

CHAPTER 6

WRONG WEATHER, CRAP CLOTHING AND RUBBISH RETAILERS:

RETAIL, CLOTHES AND FASHION

There is a fairly well-known comment that's bandied about: 'There's no such thing as bad weather, just bad clothing.'

I beg to differ, at least on the first bit (there's always bad clothing, regardless of the weather). Of course, there's bad weather … and there's horrific weather that even the most protective clothing won't be enough to save you from. But there's also poor preparation, or sometimes sheer bad luck, which is where I guess this phrase may have originated.

More than 100 years ago, natural clothing of leather, wool and animal furs failed to save Captain Robert Falcon Scott and his men as they succumbed to extreme cold on their quest to reach the South Pole. Much more recently, the film *Everest* captured the moments in 1996 when commercial climb leaders Rob Hall and Scott Fischer, along with two of their clients, were killed on their descent when their ultra-modern mountaineering clothing was sadly insufficient to protect them from protracted hostile weather.

'Bad' weather comes in many forms, and that includes too much sunshine. Previously, I suggested that sunshine is a positive, and in many ways it is. However, getting too much of virtually anything is unwise, and the World Health Organization estimates that overexposure to the sun causes some 60,000 deaths worldwide every year. In this case, too, it's inadequate clothing (and the resulting impact of intense ultraviolet light on the skin's surface) that is to blame.

The bottom line is that at times we really are at the mercy of the awesome power of the weather, particularly the extremes. If we dare to ignore it – or even challenge it, by what we choose to wear or don't wear – we stand to lose far more often than we'll win, and sometimes the stake is in human lives.

For the most part, the clothing we wear on a day-to-day basis is aligned with the weather of the day, the week or the season. Clothing retailers and the fashion industry strive to clothe us in their delights in what is a hugely competitive environment. But there's a problem, an ongoing problem that I have observed year in and year out.

The fashion calendar, which dictates when the various fashion houses show off their latest collections to their purchasing clients, usually rolls out months ahead of the seasonal calendar. The seasonal calendar hopefully then behaves itself and spring, summer, autumn and winter arrive and depart, delivering the weather they usually impart. For the most part they do: temperatures gradually rise, fall away and then rise again, and wet seasons replace dry seasons that replaced wet seasons.

But then there's the weather, and that's where things can, and do, go astray. By that I mean any season can lose its identity due to spells or periods of unusual or unanticipated weather. You know what I mean – those times in the northern hemisphere when warm southerly winds make a mockery of what's supposed to be a cold and snowy winter, as with most of the US during winter 2019/20.

Or, just as the pivotal Easter holidays kick in across Western Europe or the northeast of the US, biting north or northeast winds usher in a late wintry backlash.

The fashion houses don't so much care, as they have long since been done and dusted and are either on holiday or designing their wares for seasons to come. But for the clothing retailers, it's a different matter altogether. They live for the moment, and it doesn't matter how hard they try, unseasonal weather is their nemesis.

As I mentioned in the previous chapter on food and beverages, we the shoppers also live for the moment, and when the weather tangles itself in knots, there's no way we are going to buy clothing we'd ordinarily purchase at another time of year. Remember that little ditty of mine, referring to every drop of rain and every rise and fall in the mercury impacting supply and demand? Well, in these contra-seasonal cases, the supply ends up over-supplied and the demand ends up dead on arrival.

The sad thing here is that these unusual weather spells do happen, and when they do, they have the capacity to ruin a company's performance and torpedo their stock price. Roll out the CEO's or CFO's excuse: "It was the weather that did it!" Except, sometimes, it wasn't – it was more likely because of inaction or poor planning. At such times, it can be useful to dig deep and differentiate.

Obviously, we can't control the weather, and climate change is making things that bit more intricate.

So, what are the solutions for retailers who really do suffer at the hands of Mother Nature?

If that's you, then listen up. This is what I believe will help:

1. **Keep you finger on the weather pulse and plan accordingly.** Yes, here we are again feeling pulses, but those who neglect to look into the future, and plan, deserve nothing. So, ensure that you have a reputable source of weather forecast information, not only for the next couple of days but for the month and the season to come. The very best information isn't free, and you won't find the cream of the cream floating around on the internet. And so, if you want it, be prepared to pay for it.

2. **If necessary, employ an in-house meteorologist.** I find it unfathomable that retail companies employ all kinds of skilled and unskilled personnel to make their company *great again*, but when it comes to that aspect of business that can make or break a financial quarter or entire year, only a few employ meteorologists. Time to change that inane historic position, I venture.

3. **Be quick and be nimble.** There are no prizes for being last off the mark when the weather changes for good or ill. It's an intensely competitive world out there, and the cut of your cloth may be fantastic, but it will never see the light

of day if your competitors are shining a light on their prize assets ahead of you. And, if you're still trying to flog winter gear when the first ice cream cones are selling in the parks or on the beaches, you really are in the land of the sloths. If your wares are in the hands of a marketing firm, ensure that they follow these guidelines, because personal experience tells me many do not. I'll be tackling marketing and advertising in a chapter to come, but for now please steer well clear of the sloths.

4. **Be flexible and dance!** The weather bends, the weather changes colour, the weather changes its feathers, the weather never stands still, and no two weather days are the same. As such, you too should strive to be as flexible, bendy and colourful as possible. Be prepared to change window displays and the shop-front area. Be prepared to press the marketing button and also the stop button. In a respectable and lawful way, of course, be prepared to engage and disengage staff to meet likely demand. And finally, be prepared to wear a pair of shoes that you can dance in, because if you want to succeed you really do need to strut your stuff.

5. **Measure weather elements versus footfall and sales.** If you trade blind, then you deserve to fall down a deep, dark hole. To know the future, measure the past. OK, sales are not all about weather,

but it can influence a good part of them. If you're able to strip out the obvious and the anomalies, then applying historical weather data against footfall and sales should paint a very useful picture. Most things have a tipping point, and that includes clothing that's directly linked to the weather, such as swimwear, Wellington boots, gloves and woolly jumpers. By mapping the past, you will be able to negotiate a way forward and stay free of those dark chasms.

6. **Anticipate the mood.** If changes in the weather create opportunities, climate change affords a potential bonanza. If the world is moving toward lower-carbon-footprint foods, such as veggie burgers over beef burgers, then the same applies with clothing. After all, fashion is a mood and a desire, even a political statement. As such, I think you can make a relatively safe bet that sustainable apparel that represents a more caring and careful world will be at the forefront of fashion in the decades to come. If not, then I'll eat your furry hat!

7. **Change your face.** If you operate within bricks and mortar, then weather can sometimes be a huge hindrance in terms of footfall. Sunshine, heat, high winds, snow, ice and rain all keep the customers away. Moreover, and perhaps even more importantly, the world is changing.

Online sales have risen astronomically in recent years and mammoth department stores are heading the way of the mammoth, unless customers can be attracted to stores by something other than what they're commonly selling. Two words come to mind: entertainment and comfort. My advice is to change your face. Offer your customers a revolution in shopping entertainment; make them want to come and want to stay. Offer the comfort they need to cope with the weather of the day. You never know, you might actually sell even more than you bargained for.

CHAPTER 7

SNOWED UNDER OR RAINED OUT?: GENERAL RETAIL

OK, we've covered the absolute necessities of the weather-sensitive retail sector, which accounts for some 70% of the purchases we might make in any given year. However, there are other retail areas that are arguably even more prone to weather impacts. And, unlike basic consumption items and clothing, in these we tend to have more of a take-it-or-leave-it option, which creates greater susceptibility to the weather's many whims.

We are by and large creatures of comfort, and when the weather turns in any way negative or hostile, we tend to stay put. We're content to sit out the horribleness rather than face it down. Nowadays, from a retail perspective, that means we press plenty of buttons and ask companies to deliver stuff to our doorstep instead of driving, taking public transport or walking to the shop. Somewhat akin to Covid-19 experiences but obviously to a lesser degree, online retail, online retail sales and TV programming receive a major boost during adverse weather, while in-person footfall attendance declines commensurate with the severity of weather.

I recall an icy Friday evening in the winter of 2018, when the 'Beast from the East' had made its mark during the day, laying down a few inches of snow around the area where I live. Not the kind of snow that would normally make the news or disrupt traffic, but certainly enough to play on minds and increase fiddling with worry beads. Even though no more snow was forecast for that evening, and roads were generally passable, the fear and hesitation those few inches of white stuff created was enough to turn nearby town centres into scenes from a post-Armageddon sci-fi thriller: frigid, empty and lifeless.

Well, almost. There were a few 'lost souls' out there, including my family and me, who drove ever so easily to a French restaurant some three miles away, where we were greeted by a skeleton staff and a ghost-like atmosphere. And remember, this was a usually-busy Friday evening in what is normally a lively, bustling restaurant.

You see, weather impact might not be that apparent or disabling, but a taste of it – or even the threat of it – can be enough to severely affect the norm. That is pivotal, not only for restaurants but for a whole host of mainly leisure-oriented venues, such as cinemas, theatres, swimming pools, bowling alleys and sporting facilities. Indeed, walk along a high street or into a shopping centre, pick any outlet, and you'll observe a measurable effect. The greater the weather extreme, the greater the impact, and the drop in footfall may also have staffing implications. Indeed, you may like to view an extreme of weather a little like a small-time passing virus!

You might not think that uncommonly hot days, when the mercury rises in tandem with blood pressure, would have an equally adverse impact, but you'd be mistaken. Heat, and particularly heat with high humidity, leads to a search for comfort and pleasure, which are not so easily found in town or city centres beyond the air-conditioned outlets.

Incidentally, Europe comes in a poor third compared to the US and developed Asia when it comes to the prevalence of air conditioning. So, for some, finding the comfort of air-conditioned outlets can be a needle-in-a-haystack proposition. Instead, when the heat index climbs, people head for the beaches, parks, rivers, lakes and swimming pools.

Where there is a weather loser there's a weather winner – a phrase I will return to again and again. During days of high heat, cooling breezes and even cooler stretches of water attract humans like bees to a honeypot. In that I have first-hand, recent experience.

Unless the record has been beaten again since this book was published, on 29 July 2019 the UK hit its highest-ever recorded temperature: 38.7 degrees Celsius (101.7 Fahrenheit). At the time, I was sitting in the café of my local park, within a tree-lined leisure complex, complete with a gym and outdoor swimming pools. While I was there the gym remained more or less empty, but the queues for the swimming pool were out the door and into the middle of the park. It was even necessary for the staff to provide water for those biding their time, and wilting, in the unprecedented heat.

Inside the café, cold drinks and ice cream were consumed to the point of running out, with several hours of open time still to go. Bottom line: all of these water-seeking refugees were not in the town centre, nor were they in the cinemas, furniture stores, computer outlets or DIY centres that are replicated in every village, town and city. Populations were driven in herds to refreshing water sources, not unlike thirsty wildebeest in the middle of an African dry season.

It was, in short, bonanza time for selected retailers of cooling comfort ... and a barren, unforgiving desert for most others.

That summer, the oldest holiday tour operator in the UK fell afoul of the heat as the British flocked to British beaches, instead of foreign ones. That may have been the straw that broke the camel's back, as long-term mismanagement and Brexit uncertainties were blamed for the company's fall into receivership. Nonetheless, the tour company could fairly be called a weather loser.

Speaking of hot weather, let's turn to a classic situation where hay may be made by the baleful – that is, when a heatwave ends with a literal bang. You can guess the scenario: a big city centre in a temperate climate zone, 20 days of blistering sunshine and outlandish media hype, and then the epic thunderstorm arrives.

Who could possibly be the weather winner in that situation? Well, it's the guy who sought out, noted and trusted a reliable weather forecast in the days before, and bought a crate of umbrellas at wholesale. The guy who then sold them at a premium to those poor drenched individuals, scurrying from door to door, who hadn't sorted or noted or trusted anything, or perhaps chose the wrong forecast to rely upon.

There are of course countless examples of 'capturing the moment' at the top of the retail weather-impact iceberg. But like every iceberg, the bulk of the script lies under the water line. If you sell something, think for a minute of how every type of weather may or may not lean heavily upon your business. The impacts may shift like the blowing sands of the Kalahari, but there are few, if any, businesses that can claim to be totally weather resistant.

Take undertakers, for example. The business of human burial is a form of retail, but hardly something we think about very often. It certainly doesn't spring to mind as clinging to the top of that weather-impact iceberg. But the next time you chat with an undertaker, ask whether weather materially impacts their business. The answer will be a resounding yes, or at least it should be. Just go back to the chapter on health and wellbeing to see that fatalities during weather extremes can climb to the top of that iceberg faster than a penguin!

Then there are hairdressers. Again, not the most obvious of weather-impacted merchants, but as the air turns colder, we tend to wear our hair longer, as a way of keeping our head and neck warm. Hot weather makes us want to reduce our hair mass for reasons of comfort. September is actually one of the most popular months for going to the hairdresser, though not quite as popular as December, when people want to get ready for Christmas. That's in part due to summer (especially for women) being a time of throwing your hair up and embracing a more natural beach vibe, as the sun, heat and humidity make your tresses difficult to maintain. Once the cool of early autumn arrives, women flock to the salon to restyle their hair and embrace a more maintained look. There's certainly method to all this madness.

And, of course, there are times when hostile weather makes for panic buying of certain basic 'survival items.' Hurricanes or typhoons can see supermarkets and DIY stores stripped of items such as tea, coffee, sugar, bread, tins of beans, wooden boarding, torches, candles and generators. Petrol stations do big business at these times too, not only in increased fuel sales for those wishing to escape, but as an open-all-hours convenience store for those opting to stay put.

The list goes on and on, but it's fair to say that every item and every retail operation has its time, its place and its value commensurate with the antics of Mother Nature.

CEOs, business owners, operations professionals and demand managers, you know your business, and I probably don't. But I do know about the immense impact weather can have, and what counts ... and with all due respect, you might not, or at least not have the full story. All businesses, whether retail or not, should factor in weather, alongside every other business-critical equation.

So, be mindful of where you source your weather information. Learn to recognize precisely what parts of the business can be impacted by which types of weather, and when, by observing and/or measuring it. Where possible, be fleet of foot and diversify – it's not by accident that chocolate bar manufacturers diversified into chocolate ice cream as global temperatures started their steep rise during the 1990s. And finally, build in contingencies for all types of weather, particularly those ever-increasing extremes.

Become weather-impact savvy, learn to become a weather winner, and donate the loser's medal to your competitors.

CHAPTER 8

FEEL THE PULSE AND PRESS THE BUTTON:
ADVERTISING AND MARKETING

As we know from the opportunistic umbrella seller in the middle of New York's Times Square on the first wet weekend in a blue moon, being there – and being seen as filling a pressing need – is a necessary part of the marketing and advertising of just about everything.

You might be harbouring the best thing since sliced bread, demand for which is sure to outstrip the supply. It could be a 'thing' that is so acutely weather-sensitive that, on the right day, it becomes invaluable to those who'd simply have to have it.

However, if your 'thing' is kept in a cupboard, if you don't shine a light on it at the opportune moment and flog it for all it's worth, you might as well give it up. You knew that, of course, but it's always worth being reminded of. Even the best marketers sometimes don't see the wood for the trees. (Did I say sometimes? I actually meant often!)

In the previous three chapters we learned about the umbilical cord that connects the commercial world to every nuance of the weather. It really doesn't matter what line of business or service we're talking about, because monitoring the weather is absolutely essential. That's not only the case on the day in question, but over several days in advance, in order to achieve the best possible synergy between a product or service and the weather your target audience experiences.

It would also be useful to keep one eye on social moods, fashions and the latest popular culture whims, relative to climate change, because the world is changing, and marketers must follow the scent in order not to be left holding yesterday's baby. Yet, with a few exceptions – mostly weather-savvy US companies – in practice, marketers appear far too busy to engage at a focused, professional level.

As you know, I call the art and science of weather monitoring 'feeling the pulse' – it's about keeping tabs on the weather's many moods, if you like. I'll go much deeper on this in the areas of sport, financial trading and insurance, in the chapters ahead because, in those industries, weather tracking can be absolutely critical. But in this chapter, allow me to focus on weather-related marketing as a general tool for all and sundry.

Once a product or service has a known weather link, and in particular if there are weather elements that are likely to drive or sink sales, then the timing of any promotion's launch and end-date are the keys to success. All too often I've witnessed businesses of all types *react* to changes in the weather, as opposed to being proactive and getting their message out there ahead of their opponents. You see, the early bird really does catch the worm when it comes to weather-related sales.

Worse still, there are businesses that arrive very late on the scene with their promotions, and fail to pull them when the supporting weather type breaks. What an unnecessary waste of time, energy and money!

And then there are those businesses and services that, frankly, don't bother at all. They believe they're weather resistant, or that the elements only have a minimal impact upon them. Sure, there are businesses that in the general sense of things are at the bottom of the weather-sensitivity iceberg or volcano, but opportunities can still arise when the weather is particularly extreme.

Consider the banking or accounting industries, which hardly shake flippers with that iceberg-climbing penguin in the previous chapter. Yet, both of these industries have numerous clients who *are* weather sensitive. In dealing with them, supportive texts, messages, emails and other timely promotional messages could be sent. Opportune talks or seminars concerning the subject in hand might be arranged, as in times of severe weather attributed to climate change. We all like to be well-in-formed, and banks, accountants and other business-ori-entated sectors could gain valuable PR by having the will to act while the iron is hot.

I was once retained by a bowling alley company during a hot spell to put my name on a weather-related advertise-ment that publicized their air-conditioned venue. I guess they saw a weather guy as the ideal person to be talking heat relief. I've also assisted in promoting snow boots, a hay fever remedy, holidays in the sun, an adventure park and an insurance product.

The bottom line here is that individuals or brands with strong connections to the weather could be a valuable aid in the promotion of weather-sensitive products and services by solidifying the link. That person need not be a meteorologist; they could be an actor who starred in a weather-related film or play, or a singer with a relevant song, or indeed anybody with a positive weather or climate association.

Simply connect the dots with the appropriate person, feel the pulse and press the 'go' button.

Given that our weather experiences are often directly felt within the body, and in turn pester the mind, it follows that 'suggestive marketing' can be a powerful tool. Imagine spectators on a boiling hot day at a sports stadium, suddenly presented with adverts for ice-cold beverages, dripping their salvation down the side of the glass. Or picture the same stadium on a frigid, windy evening, with rain turning to sleet and spectators freezing their extremities off. That hot cup of cocoa being splashed across the big screens suddenly feels like a godsend ... if only to take hold of the cup to warm numb, wind-chapped hands.

Turning from products to services, in protracted icy weather, pipes tend to burst on the thaw rather than the freeze, so plumbers could benefit by timing their marketing campaigns to coincide with the day when temperatures rise a few degrees above freezing and pipes spring their leaks.

Meanwhile, builders and craftsmen might well benefit by making themselves known prior to a major storm, both in terms of useful advice and actual fix-'em-up services. If the forewarning opportunity is missed, then just after the event, when pieces are being picked up, can be a good second best, although by then the competition will be on the move too.

This thinking applies to many, many more services. Consider hospitals and doctor's surgeries, who could send out advisories on preventative measures when certain weather conditions arise. For instance, they can flag the likelihood of certain illnesses or accidents and suggest how to avoid them. Or, how about golf courses highlighting 'perfect' playing conditions, or even purveyors of the 'sunshine tablet' (vitamin D) in the middle of a dull, dank winter spell.

You see, comfort or safety factors are big catalysts for action when it comes to weather-related exposure. Believe me, it's far easier to receive a positive response when lust, fear, need, greed or anxiety are in the air. Enter coronavirus and toilet rolls!

So, feel that pulse for all its worth, and be ready to press the button!

CHAPTER 9

IT'S THE
WEATHER,
STUPID!:
THE ECONOMY
AND FINANCIAL
TRADING

It's an indisputable fact that the weather can affect the economy of a country, or an entire region, for good or bad. But, the economy cannot affect day-to-day weather. So, which is more important? Do we think about the economy every day of our lives, like we do the weather?

I'd venture to say that we don't, unless the economy happens to be *the personal economy* of money in your wallet, or when a financial crisis hits.

In my mind, short-term weather is a vital cog in the economic merry-go-round, and long-term climate is arguably becoming even more manifest. On the other hand, it's also safe to say that capitalism per se has, to one degree or another, fostered man-made climate change, and right now capitalism is in a mad scramble to undo some of the damage … for a price, of course.

Let's go back to basics. It's not by accident that over the past 400 years or so, when economic prowess actually began to mean something, the majority of the world's economic powerhouses resided in areas where the climate was neither too hot, too cold, too wet or too dry – or, at least, not any of those for too long. Indeed, the fiscal porridge was (or still is) just about right for many of the world's leading economies.

Of course, there are countries, such as the US and China, that straddle several climate zones, which do include hostile weather such as hurricanes, typhoons, tornadoes, bone-chilling cold, mountainous snow and unbearably hot and humid conditions. However, that hostility rarely persists year-round, and there are other parts of those vast countries that enjoy hospitable climates that allow industry and business to more easily flourish. Moreover, countries that boast a number of climatic zones actually benefit from a consequent diversity of products and services.

Of course, countries can also raise their economic status simply by what comes out of the ground, namely oil and precious minerals. Look no further for examples of that than the likes of Saudi Arabia and other Middle Eastern states. Climate is certainly not on their side, but they're fortunate in other ways.

Other countries are not so lucky in terms of what comes out of the ground or descends from the heavens. For them, economic survival is the watchword. Across Africa, Asia, Central America and elsewhere, inhospitable, unproductive or unpredictable climates, often coupled with short-term weather horrors and mismanagement and/or corruption, help produce economic basket cases.

The bottom line here is that the majority of successful economies tend to have 'helpful' climates, and much of the rest is down to natural resources, politics, good or bad management and natural disasters other than those related to climate and weather.

When it comes to the pure weather (as opposed to broader climatic) influences on the economy, we're talking relatively short-lived affairs. These range from a few hours, in the event of major storms, to somewhat longer periods when extremes of weather make the normal passage of life virtually impossible.

If the measure of a strengthening or weakening economy lies in the rise and fall of the gross domestic product (GDP), then weather events such as protracted hard winters, severe droughts, flooding or major storm damage can have a materially negative effect. There will be weather winners and weather losers at such times, and one has to watch for politicians and business leaders using the weather as a convenient excuse for poor performance.

Nevertheless, as a rule of thumb, if the weather is severe enough, GDP for the impacted quarter is likely to slip below the projected trend line. (Note that roughly 70% of GDP is driven by consumers, and even in the best of times the buying public can be as fickle as the weather.)

So, if we're agreed that weather can be a major player in economic wellbeing, how do the financial markets embrace such impacts? Well, in my spare time (of which I tend to have very little) I have been known to dabble in weather-related markets, and clients engage BWS for focused advisories. My experience has been that, as with sections of the retail industry, the financial trading world reacts more than it anticipates. Upon the announcement of quarterly results by a company that has been weather-impacted, for better or worse, its stock price may move wildly, although it had been stable or heading upward.

That begs the question, what precisely are analysts and traders looking at – or, more likely, *not* looking at – to have not advantageously positioned themselves ahead of the earnings announcement?

For example, a very mild winter will never play well for a company that sells cold weather-related goods or services. Similarly, a wet, cool summer rarely bodes well for a company whose wares leverage hot and sunny weather.

Once one is aware of the prime weather players, the next step is to assess whether the weather of the recent past has been more of a friend than an enemy for the companies in question. Everything else considered (and I'll delve into the 'everything else' bit in a moment), to be informed is to be empowered.

And then there are the weather-related commodities: things like oils, natural gas and many agricultural crops. Starting with the latter, we all know how weather-dependent the likes of corn, coffee, soya beans, oranges, cocoa, sugar and cotton are. It doesn't take an agronomist to look at the mechanics of these cash crops, and then map the current weather – or better still, forecast the weather that's coming – and how one will impact the other. That is in fact the stock in trade of a slew of commodity-associated weather-forecast organizations.

Fear of (or hope for) of a certain type of weather will drive prices up or down, sometimes to a greater degree than the actual weather event itself. The fear factor can move futures markets massively, in a very short time span. For example, orange juice futures tend to rise when forecasters predict a meaningful frost across Florida's citrus-growing regions. The same could be said about predicting prolonged wet weather and its effect on US soya bean or cotton crops. In Brazil and central Africa, weather forecasting plays a similarly significant role in price fluctuations in coffee or cocoa futures.

Having said all that, I really wish it was that easy. If it was, we'd all be multi-millionaires pretty damn quickly … but of course it was never going to be that simple. I'll explain why by recounting a true-life horror story.

Many moons ago, a BWS colleague and I thought we had found an easy path to instant wealth and glory, as one will do. The thinking was simple: it involved anticipating a spike in US heating oil demand due to the onset of freezing winter weather in those heavily-populated northeastern states. We would then buy the commodity on a spread-betting platform, before everybody else discovered the emerging treasure chest.

It's fair to say that there was no problem anticipating the frigid plunge when it showed itself on our modelling. And so, happy as two little lambs, on we jumped, convinced that we were ten steps ahead of the crowd.

At the time, this particular spread-betting company had pretty large spreads (the gap between buy and sell positions), and one had to have fairly deep pockets to be able to engage even at the lowest levels, which is definitely where we were. We made our move and waited for the world to catch up and start the big buy. It didn't take that long for a reaction to unfold, but it wasn't what we were expecting.

On day two, the heating oil price began to fall. By day three it wasn't just falling, it was sinking. How could this be? After all, winter was about to bite a few million bottoms very hard. Well, heating oil is very much linked to crude oil, and when crude moves, the tendency is that most other traded oils follow likewise. The problem for us was that non-weather fundamentals were at work.

Somewhere, someone (we later found out it was OPEC) was moving the goal posts, and sadly for us in the wrong direction! We clung on for another week, hoping and praying that the bloody meddling OPEC would have a change of mind, and all would come good as the snows lay thick in New York and Boston. Alas, they never did.

Between us, we lost the equivalent cost of a small new car. The mad, sad and naïve traders had certainly bit off more than they could chew!

However, within all of that, there was one mighty important lesson – one that rings true to this day. Yes, weather impacts and climate changes can and do move the financial Earth, but there are many forces beyond Mother Nature's influence that can dictate the market's ebbs and flows. Geopolitical shifts, economic factors, the moods and whims of market-controlling algorithms and even a single Tweet or indeed a devastating virus can scuttle the best-laid plans.

Financial trading is not only about playing the short-term blips and slips, because the majority of traders look long term. And so, monthly and seasonal weather outputs are seriously important. A seasonal peak or trough in a certain commodity or stock for weather-related reasons will not stay at the same level if *pure* weather is the driver, simply because the weather flows up and down. It does so as much, if not more, than those wavy financial graphs that nearly always lead back to square one, eventually.

Looking even further ahead, and with climate change increasingly becoming a major market-impacting factor, it may pay for you to take a good look at new or relatively new companies that are integral to offsetting climate change in one way or another. I don't know how these mostly US companies are going to perform in the years to come, but Beyond Meat (a producer of plant-based meat substitutes) and Generac Inc (a backup-power generation supplier for when the lights *really* go out), are two that fit the bill. There are of course many others out there to tickle your fancy.

There are no panaceas here either, but after the final chapter you may want to refer back to this one.

Finally, before executing any weather-related trade, it pays to aggregate as much relevant information as possible.

Utilize the skills and expertise of a financial advisor and a savvy meteorologist, if necessary, to help ensure that you're on a firm footing.

It bears repeating that nothing is guaranteed; nothing can be. But trading, like sports betting, is all about edges and being *one* step ahead of the crowd – not necessarily ten!

CHAPTER 10

THE *REAL* 12TH MAN:
INSIDE SPORT

Sport, in all its forms, is about discovering the same edges I've mentioned in retailing and financial trading ... at least if being competitive and winning is the name of the game.

That means finding the extra inch, the extra mile, the extra bit of this or bit of that, in order to prosper, all while overcoming the inevitably well-edged opposition.

Along the way, any sport that's inherently open to the elements has to deal with them, or make use of them, which can throw up an extraordinary number of obstacles and opportunities.

At this point, allow me to declare not only my lifelong active interest in sport generally, but also my long association with sports teams of many shades and colours, over many years, as an amateur, professional and otherwise. That includes not only the sports themselves, but also involvement with several sports betting companies, an area I'll cover in depth in the next chapter.

But let us begin where, for most of us, sport first enters into our lives. We've all been there, that freezing cold, wind-blown, sleety day at school, when whatever sport we were engaged in came a poor second to 'survival.' Likewise, it could have been a boiling hot and humid day, when running a mile seemed like a several hundred steps too far, with mind and body sagging under the oppressive heat.

The truth is, those extreme days really were more like a test of character, durability and endurance. But the elements need not be all that excessive to impact a particular sport. Indeed, even the best of days can be a blessing or a curse for teams and individuals alike, in terms of tactics, performance and outcomes.

For example, a lovely, warm summer's day with a little sunshine and no more than a breath of wind would for the most part tend to suit the out and out favourite. One way for the outsider in a two-way contest to stand a better chance of winning any sport would be for the weather to be such that it nullifies the more honed skills of the favourite. That would generally involve high-impact weather such as hard rain, high winds, snow, mud and other unsavoury stuff. It's called a 'leveller,' and managers and coaches of inferior teams or lowly-ranked individuals should spend a few minutes every week praying to their god, the sky or their eyelids for the weather to be offside, so they can be onside.

My initial amateur dabble in sport as an adult came when I scuffed my way through to a couple of English Football Association junior/youth coaching badges and became a coach and manger of various teams up to the age of 18. That period spanned almost 20 years, and I used the weather to my advantage on countless occasions.

I was well aware of what was coming weather-wise, so the first step was to prepare the team for their encounter with the elements. That involved simple things, like wearing appropriate clothing and consuming an appropriate diet to deal with the conditions. Still, there was nothing worse as a coach than a team of youngsters moaning and groaning about being too cold, too wet or too hot when their focus was supposed to be on the game.

However, the real advantage was to be able to use the weather conditions tactically. That might have been as simple as playing the second half with the opposition blinded by an ebbing sun, or, in a wet game with a soggy pitch, playing direct football, which involves hoofing the ball instead of dribbling or passing short.

High winds were always the most difficult to master. So long as the wind was to be consistent throughout the game, my cunning plan was to play the first half with the wind in our faces, simply because we were fresh and able to cope with the onslaught better than we would with tired legs in the second half. These small tweaks often worked, sometimes they didn't, but in sport – as in weather – there is no sure thing. We'll talk more about that shortly.

Weather impact in sport is not all about football, although it is the most complex of sports in terms of studying and understanding precisely how a coach could take advantage of prevailing conditions. So much so, in fact, that I developed a seminar intended to educate and offer an advantage to football clubs and associations. There have been few takers, but it's true that change in football tends to happen very slowly!

So, turning to the wide array of other weather-sensitive sports, there can be none more prone than cricket. If it rains, there's usually no play happening, and in most forms of the game the draw then looms larger. However, in the 20-over game, I have often seen umpires brave the elements in order to arrive at a result. But that's an exception to the rule, and more often than not in the one-, four- or five-day versions of the game, win the toss and you win the match. Or, win the toss, make a poor pitch, or a questionable weather-related batting or fielding decision, and watch the egg splatter all over embarrassed red faces.

Bottom line: in cricket, any captain worth their salt needs to feel the weather pulse every bit as keenly as retailers, traders, construction workers, farmers and other acutely sensitive professionals.

Let's talk about golf, which is certainly weather dependent. With every breath of wind the ball moves this way and that, tilting the golfer from success to failure and back again. Add in rain, a wet course, high humidity and temperature extremes, and we have 'the perfect storm.' Not sure how many of the top professionals employ meteorological observers, if any, but perhaps they should, as the vital edges may be numerous.

How about fishing? It's common knowledge that fish tend not to bite after rain, and windy days also diminish the chances of snapping jaws. Fish are pretty savvy when it comes to detecting and acting upon various weather phenomena, such as air pressure changes, storms, freezes and heat-waves. They've been around for far longer than us, and oceanographic and meteorological factors are imprinted within their DNA. Fishermen would always do well to study the habits of the species they're hoping to snare.

I guess I could go on and on about how weather impacts the sporting world, across the board. For instance, I spent a couple of years assisting a now-defunct Formula One Grand Prix team (the defunct bit wasn't my fault, honest!). I then spent a couple more years out in the field, lending my expertise to a top world rally outfit. Believe me, weather, particularly rain, was an absolutely critical factor. Tracking down and monitoring individual shower clouds, just in case they spilled their goods on the track within say a 15-minute window, was something of a nightmare on occasions, and I was often tested to my limits.

American football clearly falls into the category of weather-prone sports. Extreme heat or cold, rain, snow and particularly high winds can have a real effect on the game. Have you ever thought what it must feel like for a team based in tropical Florida team to travel north to Green Bay, in the teeth of a mid-winter storm with air temperatures cold enough to freeze the breath within seconds? I know which team I'd be backing.

Then there's athletics (track and field), where we really get down to the physical and psychological effects of weather. In the chapter devoted to health and wellbeing, we learned how the weather leeches itself into our skin and literally takes over our brain functions. That certainly applies to athletes of all abilities, even top professionals. It's a given that if the weather is in any way hostile, no records will be broken, bar the wrong ones. For example, track times will tend to be slower due to wet underfoot conditions, and strong crosswinds won't help javelin or discus throwers.

Moreover, accidents and injuries are more likely than they'd otherwise be in clear conditions. Cold weather, along with the wind-chill factor, can have a huge impact on not-so-warmed hamstrings, quads and calf muscles. I've had personal experience with such a clash, and my tortured hamstring burdened me for weeks after. Extreme heat could lead to the same outcome, but I'm reliably informed that in warm conditions such pulls are more than likely due to overuse than to the weather itself.

Returning to football for a second, in the recent past I had the pleasure of chatting with a director and psychologist from the Brentford Football Club, an English Championship club with a strong passing game ... at least at the time of writing. They told me about a midweek away match they'd played against a big, brawny Sheffield United team during mid-winter.

The weather was pitiful – raw and cold, with an icy wind – and at half-time all the Brentford players were talking about was how cold they were. They were losing, and went on to capitulate further in the second half, with brawn firmly beating agility. It wasn't that the more robust physical team beat the brilliant, skinny featherweights for reasons beyond size and weight; it was actually down to mental toughness in the face of adverse weather.

And then there's road cycling, which is totally at the mercy of the elements. The 2019 Tour de France revealed that in no uncertain terms, particularly in the Alps and Pyrenees, where record French heat mercilessly turned into horrendous storms. Huge hail, floods and landslides threatening not only the order of the race, and the event itself, but actual lives and limbs. The weather-sports equation seldom reaches those nightmare levels, though sporting injuries and fatalities due to lightning strikes vie for what has to be the most undesirable trophy.

If you think that weather only affects us humans in sport, you'd be mistaken. Horses, dogs and, of course, jumping fleas are all weather-prone to one degree or another, whether we're talking weather in the air or weather that has made its mark on ground surfaces. Soft, heavy or overly firm going at racecourses is often a sound reason to pull certain horses ahead of the starting bell. In any event, if you know your horses, then the prevailing conditions should tell you what kind of performance to expect from horse A or horse B.

During heavy rain events, greyhound tracks tend to puddle up on the inside lane, making it harder for dogs to run in that part of the circuit. The dog in the outside lane clearly has the advantage, then.

Meanwhile, my thanks to a great guy from one of the UK's big-bucks betting firms, Paul Dunning of BetFred, for pointing out that although we might think indoor sports are 'weather free zones,' they aren't. Back in 1981, the English Billiards final held in the historic City of Chester was held up due to snow on the table. It seems a hole in the roof had allowed overnight snow to fill the corner pocket!

I'd like to finish this section with a little piece of advice. If you are involved in any sport where the weather plays a part, major or minor, then educate yourself, understand it, plan for it and embrace it. Protect yourself whenever necessary with appropriate clothing and footwear. In cold weather, warm your exposed muscles more than you otherwise would, and adopt a mindset that allows you to play the 12th man to your advantage, because chances are your opponent will only have 11.

Oh, and good luck. Luck is another bench player, and a close relative of the weather!

CHAPTER 11

PLACE YOUR YOUR BETS (WISELY): SPORTS BETTING

Talking of necessary luck, let's move on to sports betting. Face it, at least a little bit of luck here is always welcome. However, allow me to also add a little bit of worthwhile science to your portfolio.

Stemming from my lifelong love of sport, my coaching experiences, my professional observational skills, tons of data crunching and years of experience in supplying bookmakers, syndicates and individuals with site-specific weather updates across the sports, I feel I have a little something to offer when it comes to sports betting.

Listen up; it might just be worth a flutter!

From a professional standpoint, it all started some 20 years ago. I met a fantastic guy called Patrick Jay. At the time, he was the General Manager of Sportsbook at the UK betting firm Ladbrokes. (More recently he's been Chief Operating Officer at MoPlay, based in Gibraltar.) I fondly remember walking nervously into the Ladbrokes boardroom, and in front of a dozen or so sports traders Patrick introduced me as, "The most important man to sit in this particular room for many years."

Really? I was grateful, but somewhat taken aback, though I knew I had a new and valuable key to a door that was worth the generous praise Patrick was heaping upon me.

The rest is a long story – much longer than this book – involving thousands upon thousands of fixtures, meetings and weather forecasts carried out for individual sporting events. This led to the confirmation, and at times discovery, of many nuances of weather-related impact across various global sports. And that ultimately provided a significant edge to those who dabbled in sports betting.

But don't take my word for this marriage of (often) inconvenience. Here are a few words from Patrick himself:

"There is no professional athlete in the world who doesn't know – either consciously or unconsciously – that the climate conditions during their event impact their performance. Wet, wind, heat, cold, etc., all are important factors. The betting industry understands this, but not properly and not to the correct extent.

"By way of example, ask most odds compilers what is the number one impact on runs scored in a baseball game. They will say wind. They are wrong. It is humidity, because the denser air makes it harder for a ball to travel through the air. And wind, as we know, is unpredictable in stadium environments. Humidity is not. There are countless other 'secrets.'

"The other charge is that the market is already aware of the climatic conditions, and that's factored into the odds. I categorically state that it isn't. I have been working in sports betting for 25 years. The evidence is bulletproof. The market doesn't get what is important, and why, and to what extent.

"Finally, the weather forecasts from web sites and apps are generic. They are for tourists. You need to know the weather over the stadium, over the event, not in London. It may be raining and windy at Selhurst Park, South London (it always is), and bright, hot and sunny at Stamford Bridge, West London (it always is), but your app says rain with some sunshine for London.

"As such," Patrick said, "stadium-specific professional forecasts are a must."

Detouring away from sports for a moment, there's what's termed the 'novelty market,' which comes around once a year, with the *White Christmas* bets. You know the drill: a snowflake having to land on this city or that during the 24 hours of the big day. It's a pure, unadulterated weather bet, of course, and for the past 20-odd years I have adjudicated on behalf of certain bookmakers.

Bookies mean a lot of things to a lot of people, but they cannot be seen as judge and jury on something they aren't qualified to referee. So, it's been my job not only to count the snowflakes (or lack of them) but to also provide updates on the likelihood of snow, beginning on the first day of December. Every second year (swapping annually with one of my colleagues), my Christmas has been spent staring at precipitation radars and checking on what the professional observers are actually observing nationwide ... hoping, as they do their job, that they haven't had too much of the merry stuff!

As we discovered in the previous chapter, for good or ill, virtually every sport has its own unique relationship with the weather. A certain sport's positive weather could easily be another sport's negative weather, and it's all by degrees, sometimes very minor ones. It's by picking up on these small or larger impacts that vital edges can be gained when it comes to deciding what to bet on, when and why.

However – and this is a BIG however – let me make it plain, there are NO panaceas.

A wet and windy rugby union match might be expected to come in with low point totals, and perhaps the outsider doing better than they otherwise might. That's true, and for the most part it tends to happen that way as wet and windy weather translates to a tough-going lottery. But what happens when the outsider team gets a player sent off in the first ten minutes and the rest of the team succumb to the miserable conditions? The favourites then run riot, making any weather-related bet look like a big, wet blanket flung in your general direction.

It happens. Accept it and prepare for the next match with the same vigour and optimism.

It may not be a panacea, but massive points being scored during seriously hostile weather really is the exception to the rule. That's true not only in rugby union, but likewise in American football, lacrosse, Aussie Rules (oh yes, Aussie Rules with knobs on!), rugby league, field hockey,

Gaelic football and other team sports that often escape me, but you will know of them and how weather-prone they can be.

You might think that all of this would be common knowledge, done to death, a doddle, a shoo-in and all of that? I beg to differ. Like sports, weather is often unpredictable, and certainly at stadium level. Even the understanding of what X or Y weather actually means to a certain betting market – such as handicaps, total points, completed matches and the rest – is not fully understood, appreciated or acted upon.

The weather-sport mix can often be a heady one, a crazy one, even a chaotic one.

It's seldom easy picking out the bones from such situations, except to cite that learned quote from *Game of Thrones*, "Chaos is a ladder." So, use it! Where the sun doesn't shine, dark shadows lie, and in that dim light it's possible to make some hay.

To do that you need to know the basic weather-impact rules of any sport you may fancy dabbling in, starting with the 'no panacea' rule. Weather-related betting does not constitute putting your house, your car or your welfare on the line, nor anybody else's for that matter. As with financial trading, having the knowledge goes hand in hand with using it wisely and, within monetary limitations, knowing which moves risk nothing but the betting stake itself.

This is not a get-rich-quick scheme. I should know; I've got the knowledge and I'm not rich ... at least not in the eyes of the many.

We've already covered a couple of the basics: hostile weather can be a leveller, and points or high scores in the sports mentioned are generally hard to come by. Actually, those two pieces of knowledge alone should take you a long way, if you're armed with robust weather forecast information. Big, physical teams tend to do well in such weather, while fitter, more agile teams seem to revel in energy-sapping heat.

Point three, therefore, has to be to know your players/teams/tactics and then apply the weather of the moment. In golf, for example, would you really back a player whose major prowess is finesse around the greens, while a gale is blowing? Chances are, they will struggle to make the greens. Which brings me to another point: you don't have to back a team or an individual player; you can simply discount them from winning (lay them) if the weather conditions do not suit their style of play.

If you are really on top of the weather and well-versed in the art of radar-watching (and it definitely is an art), there's another trick to have up your sleeve. If the book-makers are clued up and behaving like sheep by following the market leaders or sports-book makers, then certain match markets may have already been adjusted. For example, total match points may have been reduced due to expected rain. But (and it happens) what if the rain clears just before kickoff, and the pitch is in a healthy state? On this occasion, the market is likely to have been reduced too far, so a buy as opposed to a sell of the total points may well be in order.

You see, bookmakers do have their fingers on the pulse, but very often it's the sports pulse alone, and once they've set their stall out, they tend to be very reluctant – or too lazy – to chase clouds.

Let's step away from the immediate pre-match moment and take a trip back a few days, or even a week, before an event starts for another little gem worthy of consideration. Cricket is the best one for this, but it applies to American Football or indeed any sport where the bookmakers post the odds up well in advance, which isn't that usual.

So, imagine a cricket test match in Adelaide, with Australia going up against Pakistan. The form suggests a comfortable home win, with the initial draw price around 8s in decimal talk, 7-1 in old money. However, your homework suggests that this match will be weather-impacted from day 1 of the 5, though it's not yet common knowledge. You place your money, and wait and watch. One thing you don't want to happen is for the weather forecast to dry up. But in truth, this is a bet to nothing, because even if it did clear up, the upward movement in the draw price would likely be small, and you could get out with just a small loss by laying the draw.

On this occasion, however, the wet weather scenario holds firm, and the hitherto disinterested home backers – and those who now see what you saw a few days earlier – leap on the draw like bees to the honeypot. The good news for you is that the weight of money forces the draw price lower and lower, to a point perhaps where you can choose to happily lay the draw with a small cover bet and be on a win-win (known as being 'all green'). Or, the happy alternative is to hold on throughout the match and hope that the rain delivers, with the teams struggling to play out to a result.

I've witnessed this near-bulletproof scenario on countless occasions over the years, and on a few of them I have ridden that opportune donkey all the way home!

Trust me, there are many ways of skinning the sports-betting cat by being on top of the weather. I'm going to end this chapter by focusing on the world's most popular, and arguably the most technical, sport: football (or soccer, if you prefer).

The reason for homing in on football is that there are countless opportunities across the diverse spectrum of daily matches. There's that, and the fact that along with my own personal coaching experiences, my colleagues and I at BWS have studied the weather impacts in detail ... and in this, there is a method to the madness.

I am reliably informed that bookmakers make up the football markets by assessing the following key criteria:

- Form
- Head-to-head
- Historical statistics
- The referee
- The marketplace (weight of bets)
- Maths versus positional value

In terms of the markets, there are six majors that are driven by these six factors:

1. Win probability
2. Goal expectation
3. Corner expectation
4. Card expectation
5. Player score expectation
6. Penalties

Except in the criteria list, there is a missing *seventh heaven* of course: weather impact. For reasons I've already mentioned, and others, the vast majority of bookmakers do not incorporate weather into their odds equations, which kind of leaves an open goal for savvy punters.

It's fair to say that some 80% of matches played across any given year will not be weather prone; the weather will not be impactful enough to materially change the outcome of any of the listed markets. But that still leaves a massive 20% to engage with, one way or another.

When we crunched the data, we did so over several seasons and across five major European leagues. The results did vary from league to league and from season to season, a bit like the weather changes from day to day and season to season. But there were several consistencies, which we then designed our forecast based-database around. We aptly named it WIDE (Weather Impact Deviation Expectation).

WIDE was designed to predict the deviations away from the values arrived at by the six-fold market criteria. For example, a match with a slick or wet pitch, due to in-play rain or drizzle, would be corrected to increase goal totals to between 0.4 and 0.6 per game. A seriously hot and humid match would deviate downward by up to 1.0 goals per game. Those deviations may not sound like much, but in betting terms they are huge movements.

Our WIDE deviations account for match handicaps, total goals, cards, penalties and corners, but in the right hands it may be possible to take the deviations into individual player performances. (Remember Brentford FC and those frigid players?)

I'd like to be able to open all of the data up to the masses, but I guess that would be an own goal too. Just for you, though, I'll share ten main expectations that might arise if you wait around for the 20% of matches that experience the weather's influence.

1. Any form of high-octane hostile weather, but particularly high wind, tends to be a leveller. Consider backing the underdog, more than you might otherwise.

2. Freezing temperatures and/or a freezing wind-chill factor will tend to subdue the game, and the chances of goals reduce accordingly. In frigid weather, even the physical properties of the ball toughens-up, and consequently its speed through the air reduces.

3. Hot temperatures, particularly with high humidity values, will again tend to slow the game and the goal expectations. However, the fittest teams will benefit, even if the ball swerves more in the 'thicker' air. Hot, humid weather can also be the catalyst for red and yellow cards (hot heads and all that).

4. Rain or drizzle adding to the slickness of the pitch usually results in more goals, more penalties and more cards. I've lost count of the number of wet Manchester days when City ran riot in the rain!

5. Windy days may be a leveller, but if the wind is blowing from one goal mouth to the other, then team A will benefit in the first half and team B in the next. Bet accordingly.

6. Puddled rainwater – or better still, accumulated snow – slows the ball across the surface and tends to slow the game. Physical teams or long-ball merchants prosper.

7. Acute climate differentials between the competing teams' home grounds, including altitude (air pressure differences), play out negatively on the travelling team.

8. The state of the pitch can be every bit as important as the weather in the air. Weather-hit pitches that look and play like turnip fields will not help the eloquent.

9. If the weather is benign, then forget weather entirely and concentrate on every other aspect of the game. Favourites usually prosper (form dictates, etc.).

10. Remember: there are no panaceas. Individual matches can, and do, have a will of their own. The advice I offer is no more than an edge … but fine edges can of course be very sharp!

CHAPTER 12

CHASING THE RAINBOW:
RAINBOW:
LEISURE
PURSUITS

Leisure accounts for an increasingly significant part of our lives. Indeed, more time is now devoted to leisure activities than at any other point in history. And so, given the huge influence of weather on our pastimes, this chapter becomes a little more important than it would otherwise be.

Before I go any further, the title of this chapter is meant to depict our craving for pleasure – those pursuits that make us feel good, even if it doesn't feel all that pleasurable at the time. For any actual rainbow chasers out there, you're welcome to your pastime or profession, although there is of course no pot of gold at the end of a rainbow. (Physics dictates that you can never reach the end of a rainbow, much as you can never reach the visible horizon.)

Speaking of rainbow chasers, I've long admired the group of chancers who call themselves 'storm chasers.' If I hadn't made that left turn in life, I may well have taken the right fork right and ended up in the back of an equipment-packed Jeep, careering across the American plains in pursuit of tornadoes … for the sheer thrill of it, but also to perform some useful task for the scientific world or even the media.

It's a perilous and arguably silly pursuit, and chasers have been known to fall victim to these unpredictable monster storms. It takes a rare mix of atmospheric conditions for tornadoes to form and flourish, but any engagement with these beasts is more often than not short, frantic and terrifying.

Speaking of acute weather-facing pursuits, I had a very scary experience while serving in the Royal Navy at Cumberland Bay, South Georgia. The scene: a mountainous backdrop, a huge glacier pushing its snout into the icy but crystal clear Southern Ocean, and the support ship I was stationed on, peacefully anchored in the tranquil bay on a quiet, moonlit evening.

Out of the blue, a fierce katabatic wind – which pushes high-density air downward with extraordinary force – came barrelling down the glacier. At first it was tolerable, but within minutes it was blowing at over 70mph and violently swinging our anchored ship as if it were a toy on a string.

With rugged rocks within spitting distance, there was palpable panic on the ship's bridge ... and rippling through my body, as I was supposed to be in charge of the wind, after all! And then, just as fear and embarrassment were on the verge of paralyzing me, the air pressure differential from mountaintop to sea level, which had caused the wind to happen in the first place, equalized out. Thankfully, within a couple of minutes everything (including my bodily functions) returned to normal.

That unforgettable episode has nothing to do with leisure, and even less to do with choice, but in most walks of life our down time generally has choice written all over it, with 'weather impact' boldly stamped on the packet it comes in. Unless the prevailing weather is a danger to life, or prevents travel to an intended destination, all indoor pursuits are more or less weatherproof. It's the mainly outdoor pursuits that the weather has governance over, and where choice, threat and danger continually intermix.

Whether we decide to pursue a venture or not based on the weather of the moment is common in our everyday lives. It usually starts when we first gaze out of the window or check out the forecast. The pleasures of a day trip to the coast or a walk in the woods will be amplified many times over if the weather is compliant at the outset and stays that way. If not, then other destinations will invariably be planned, and the cinemas, theatres or similar such comfort zones will benefit.

Certainly, the search for our own pleasure rainbow will extend far and wide, and from a commercial perspective there will be weather winners and weather losers whatever the weather type.

Then there are those pursuits that many of us might grin and bear, regardless of what the weather throws up. If you have a ticket to a game your favourite team is competing in, rotten weather will make for fewer bums on seats, but by and large your heartfelt passion will outweigh most forms of adverse weather. And then, it's simply a case of dressing appropriately for the occasion and taking it full in the face!

The same could be said of any kind of event or pursuit that inspires dedication or devotion, so long as the weather is not a clear and present danger. Then, even through gritted teeth, we tend to pursue our dreams ... and the dream-makers make it happen for us, because that's what they do.

But what if a certain type of weather is required to make the pastime happen at all? We've all been there and endured the frustration. After all, a mountain with no snow is hardly a skier's paradise, and what's an ocean sailing event with zero wind? A planned afternoon of sunbathing can't happen if thick cloud cover prevails, while bird spotting or stargazing might be problematic in pea soup fog.

What's happening here, and for countless other weather-dependent pursuits, is that Mother Nature is making the decision for us. She's in near total command and we are but tiny pieces in her game, to be manipulated at her will.

But, to a small degree, we are bending the rules of engagement and attempting to show that we aren't completely helpless. Humankind is very inventive, and while we are a long way from controlling the weather to any degree that matters, we are getting better at changing the nature of the game.

For example, snowmaking machines have been a godsend for ski resorts grappling with climate change. And why bother with drought-ridden canyons when man-made watercourses fulfill the needs of kayakers and canoeists?

At the same time, groundskeepers are increasingly turning away from natural grass, replacing it with materials that can withstand the ravages of weather that could put pay to an event.

Nonetheless, we still have a long way to go, and the vast majority of weather-dependent pursuits don't do 'artificial.' Yet, as climate change digs in and Mother Nature's smile ever wanes, we'll have no choice but to become that much more inventive.

As I have said, leisure is largely about choice, and even when the weather is not the be-all and end-all, as it is in many pastimes, sometimes that choice can be rudely taken from us by dangerous weather situations. That danger comes in many forms and it can arrive with little warning.

A leisurely stroll around the golf course can come to an abrupt end when thunderstorms prowl the links. The same could be said of outdoor activities like swimming, boating, hill-walking, and even car boot sales, when lightning threatens to spark. Lightning strikes may well be at the apex of dangers, but flash floods, huge hail, sudden blizzards, ice, forest fires and heatwaves have wreaked havoc with our leisure pursuits since they were first pursued.

Occasionally, we purposely place ourselves in harm's way. Extreme sports often take place where the weather can be part and parcel of the extreme. Man versus weather is a long-standing and ceaseless conflict, more often than not playing out in challenging climate zones such as mountain ranges, ferocious oceans, hot deserts and impenetrable forests. Like storm chasing, such pursuits test us to our limits, and sometimes beyond, all in the name of 'leisure.'

If that's your thing, I offer no judgment or criticism whatsoever. Whatever the risk, leisure is a huge and necessary part of our lives. But remember, whether it's a walk in the park or a clamber up a rock face, a few minutes of breaststroke at an outdoor pool or swimming the English Channel, weather will be your guide, your friend, your partner or your scourge.

CHAPTER 13

"I'M SINGING IN THE RAIN": FILM AND THE ARTS

Coming in a close second to the subject of love, weather evokes emotion, elicits imagination, inspires creativity and is deep within our souls. And, as with love, we must and do express that through the many forms of art available to us.

In this chapter, I'll explore how weather has integrated itself into all forms of art throughout the ages.

Let's begin by putting pen to paper, or rather paint to cave walls. While most cave paintings don't dwell on weather itself – beyond depictions of the sun, wildlife within weather and prehistoric man's own dress codes – it's easy to match them with the climate at the time. Cave dwellers largely painted what was important to them or what was around them, which for the most part meant what they hunted or venerated.

Thousands of years later, we can look back at such paintings and judge how the climate might have changed at a particular location. It's as good as a deep soil or ice sample, and a perfect example of climate representation from mankind's earliest times.

But it doesn't end on cave walls. Whether on stone, papyrus, paper, canvas or other surfaces, the depiction of weather in picture form has appeared from dimly lit caves and rock art right through to modern day photographs, graffiti and now social media. Very often, what was shown captured pivotal moments, such as the weather play during or following volcanic eruptions, storms, floods and major snow events. Yet, some of the most famous depictions of weather have been scenes of serenity and calmness.

The weather has provided creative inspiration for all kinds of shapes, colours, shades and moods – far too many to itemize. So, I'll stick to three of my many favourites, and hopefully you can go on to fill the huge gaps I've left.

1. **Global Warming**, by Blu, circa 2010. A huge street art mural of an hourglass containing a melting iceberg, dripping onto a flooding city below, painted onto what looks like a lift shaft wall of an office block in Berlin. It's imaginative, stark and wholly thought-provoking. 'Time running out' is the ominous suggestion.

2. **Complete Stop**, by Gregory Thielker, 2008. This is an absolute masterpiece, more like a photograph than a painting, depicting rain adorning a windowpane, obscuring the dimly-lit shapes of houses and cars in the darkness beyond. There's something comforting in this (being on the right side of the window, that is), but the raindrops, streaks and splashes give it true life that we have all witnessed once upon a time.

3. **The Magpie**, by Claude Monet, 1869. I could not trawl through weather depictions without chasing down a covering of snow, of which there are countless examples. This simple oil painting

– showing a snowy landscape, with a lone Magpie perched on a rickety wooden gate against a backdrop of a farmhouse and a few gaunt, snow-laden trees – leaves me not knowing whether to feel comforted or chilled. That's precisely what snow and ice scenes can do as they explode with exquisite majesty or harsh severity … depending on how warm and comfy you feel at the time!

Let's move on to film and television, including advertisements and social media output.

Putting my professional hat on for a second, it's been my privilege over the years to assist with television and advertising productions. I've done so both from a global forecasting perspective and a weather insurance verification angle, representing the insurers and the insured as an independent referee of unwanted things that fall from the sky, such as rain and snow. How important can this be to production companies? Many in fact take out weather-related insurance, because the wrong weather at the wrong time can be a very costly exercise that literally eats up the budget.

No matter the nature of the production, weather can be a maker or a breaker of the visual output. The breaker for me is when I watch something that purports to show real weather, but it ends up falling short or showing a plastic face. For example, snow that obviously isn't snow, or a supposedly freezing day but the breath of the actors cannot be seen. Then there's fake-looking, fake-sounding thunderstorms, high winds that look like what they really are (fan-generated moving air) and conjured-up storms that take me back to the days of string puppets, plastic sets and disorganized mayhem. Badly done weather portrayals can undermine the entire production.

On the other hand, there are productions where the weather really was core and gripped you from the inside out. For that, production companies have to make you feel that the weather is biting, burning, harassing, distressing, nurturing or warming you. Think about those films and television programmes that made you feel like you were alongside the characters, embracing or suffering the weather of the moment. It can be like the unnerving feeling you get watching a horror film, only this is pure weather and not frighteners.

The following are six productions that for me rang particularly true-to-life. I'm sure if you think hard enough you'll come up with your own weather-inspired favourites.

1. *The Revenant*, 2015: Filmed entirely in the wilds of Canada, the US and Argentina. A truly epic 'feel the deep cold and shiver' production, with stoic endeavour and heavyweight realism in the bone-chilling snowfields. Deserving of the many awards it received.

2. *Game of Thrones*, 2011-2019: The much-awarded TV series captured the very essence of weather impact, spanning several years. Filmed in the

snow-bound remoteness of Iceland, the rainy, grey skies of Belfast and the warm, sunny retreats of Morocco, the Dalmation coast and Spain, the storyline foretells an impending perpetual winter, with a bunch of dead things that were bent on bringing it. "Winter is coming." It certainly was!

3. **Walkabout**, 1971: It all started very aptly for me, in this iconic survival film, when some children find a stray weather balloon in the searing dry heat of outback Australia. Complete with an Aborigine companion, desert wildlife, buzzing flies and a blazing sun, it was difficult not to feel that you were suffering this tense walkabout with them.

4. **Gorky Park**, 1983: Although supposedly set in frigid Moscow during the depths of winter, this thriller was actually shot in the equally frozen cites of Stockholm and Helsinki. With bodies under the ice and all that, it was certainly real enough to send an icy shiver down my spine, and it's stayed long in my memory.

5. **The Perfect Storm**, 2000: Perhaps not so perfect in terms of critical reviews, but the special effects of this mighty Atlantic tempest were special enough and real-looking enough to have audiences gripping their seats and reaching for the sick bags. An excellent visual portrayal of a tragic event.

6. *The Thing*, 1982: A tense and horrific realization of the freezing and desolate isolation of Antarctica during deepest winter, complete with a defrosted angry beast of an alien. Desperate weather and desperate stakes; one to freeze your cockles off.

The starting point for all cinematic efforts tends to be a novel, non-fiction book or script. Addressing hot topics such as love, friendship, pain and death, these works – and all forms of poems, prose and rhymes – have expertly (or otherwise) portrayed the weather over many hundreds of years.

Look no further than the poet Dylan Thomas's *A Process in the Weather of the Heart*, which brilliantly combines human emotions with the weather. In T. S. Eliot's *The Love Song of J. Alfred Prufrock*, the poet describes fog akin to a cat – being quiet, stealthy and invading places most others cannot reach.

Meanwhile, there are many novels with weather well and truly entwined within the pages. *Wuthering Heights* and *The Lord of the Rings*, for example, lasso us into worlds where weather is not only pivotal to the storylines, but it rises up time and time again to make the reader feel the pleasure or the torment being endured by the characters.

I first read *The Lord of the Rings* while in the Royal Navy, sailing around the cold and windswept seas between the Falklands and South Georgia in the Southern Ocean.

It was a perfect fit; raw weather and unforgiving land-scapes were all around me, in my book, in my mind and in my bed!

Let's move on up to the sound of music. As with all the other forms of art, weather has been incorporated into the world of song and music since the first prehistoric drumbeat mimicked imminent thunderstorms. Indeed, musical instruments and the way they are played often perfectly reflect the many moods of weather.

When it comes to actual musical pieces, the classical world is alive and kicking to the sights and sounds of weather, covering everything from storms and lightning to mist and snow. I'll refrain from going overboard, but here are four that highlight the perfect marriage.

1. **'The Four Seasons,'** by Vivaldi, circa 1723. A classic of the classics. Doesn't get any better and probably never will.

2. **'La Tempesta Di Mare, Symphony 69,'** by Haydn, 1765. As an ex-sailor I should like this a lot. I like it a bit, but others know more than me.

3. **'Storm, Four Sea Interludes from Peter Grimes,'** by Benjamin Britten, 1945. Rumbustious and daunting from the downbeat; I wouldn't want to be caught in this particular storm!

4. **'Hymn to the Rising Sun,'** by Patrik Almkvisth, 2017. An epic piece of music, which captures the majesty and importance of the sun as it rises on a new day.

Beyond the classical repertoire, where would you like to start with weather-inspired popular music of the past 100 years?

Just sit back for a minute or two, and without glancing at what's below, see if you can roll off five songs that are about weather or climate, or contain pivotal weather-related passages. If you know your songs, you won't falter because there are so many. Start now!

For my part, I've chosen ten weather-related songs and three that address climate change. Feel free to look them up, listen and enjoy.

WEATHER:

1. **'Somewhere Over the Rainbow,'** by Murray Cutter, as performed by Judy Garland, 1939. Amusing, cute and hopeful.

2. **'I'm Singing in the Rain,'** as performed by Gene Kelly, 1952. Somewhat tongue in cheek, but happy-go-lucky and totally memorable.

3. **'Hazy Shade of Winter,'** by Simon and Garfunkel, 1966. A painting turned into a song, if you get my drift.

4. **'Here Comes the Sun,'** by The Beatles, 1969. Uplifting, bright and critically acclaimed.

5. **'Mr Blue Sky,'** by the Electric Light Orchestra, 1977. A joyful and bouncy finale to a concerto of weather-related songs.

6. **'Ride Like the Wind,'** by Christopher Cross, 1979. A song that uniquely evokes the presence and power of the wind.

7. **'It's Raining Again,'** by Supertramp, 1982. A perfect song for a rain-filled day, coming on the heels of other rain-filled days.

8. **'It's Raining Men,'** by The Weather Girls, 1983. Far from a favourite of mine, but it makes the list just because of the title and band name.

9. **'Weather with You,'** by Crowded House, 1992. A playful song bestowing the importance of *always* taking the weather with you. Good advice, I venture!

10. **'Echoes in the Rain,'** by Enya, 2015. A somewhat haunting theme, but at the same time hopeful and inspirational.

CLIMATE CHANGE:

1. **'When You Gonna Learn,'** by Jamiroquai, 1993. Another powerful and very apt environmental message ... and pretty funky at that.

2. **'Earth Song,'** by Michael Jackson, 1995. An indomitable song and video, with extreme climate and environmental messages.

3. **'The Seed,'** by Aurora Aksnes, 2019. Powerful, poignant and pointed. A no-bars song and video at a pivotal moment in our times.

So, the next time you venture out, remember to ride like the wind, always take the weather with you ... and if it happens to rain, grab a brolly and sing and dance like crazy!

THERE AND BACK AGAIN:
TRAVEL, TRANSPORT
AND TOURISM

Let's face it, we travel a lot. As a species we nearly always have, and we travel in various ways. So, let's briefly delve into the three Ts – travel, transport and tourism.

Speaking of films, as we did in Chapter 13, do you recall 1987's *Planes, Trains and Automobiles*? That one could have easily made my list of weather-related movies because it showed in an amusing way how much the weather can impact and alter our travel plans, and sometimes much more.

Think for a second of all the forms of transport one might use, including the old and trusted *shank's pony* (your own two legs). Every method of getting from A to Z is prone to all types of weather, and the more extreme the greater the impact.

Lest we forget, Mother Nature has the ability to delay us, stop us in our tracks or prevent us from ever going anywhere again. Most of us get a little jumpy when the plane we're on hits a pocket of turbulence, and I personally experienced feelings beyond sickness when those tumultuous Southern Seas tossed my not-so-mighty metal ship around as if it were a matchbox.

Think of the number of automobile accidents caused by ice, rain, snow, fog, wind, hail, wildfire and sun glare. (A helpful tip: if you experience heavy condensation or ice on your car's window-screen, put your visor down when you turn on the defogger and it'll clear things up so much quicker.)

I'd like to be able to offer a bunch of pointers for over-coming weather-related travel problems, but to be honest we're virtually impotent when the weather chooses to show its devilish side. But, there are still a few golden rules that should serve you well in most situations.

Rule 1. Always take the weather with you. In other words, don't neglect to avail yourself of the latest forecast, and any weather warning that may be issued, for your local area or planned route. You'll be amazed how many people simply step out without a care for what the weather professionals or transport authorities might be saying about the potential risks.

Rule 2. Plan for the worst. Depending upon the season, and what the forecasts suggest, take along things that will help you emerge from any situation unscathed. Those could include adequate footwear and clothing, appropriate food and drink, useful safety items and a means of communication. Also, if it's your own vehicle, boat or plane, see that it's made ready for the weather it's likely to face. For example, a dead battery on a cold winter's day, or an overheated engine on a hot summer's day, are the two leading reasons for motorized vehicles breaking down.

Rule 3. Don't take an unnecessary risk. If you're faced with a choice in any given situation, abide by the old saying: 'It's better to be safe than sorry.' The reason I suggest playing it safe is that trouble often arrives when the weather takes an unexpected turn for the worse and a gamble has already been taken. I won't say you should never take a risk – sometimes that's necessary, or even inevitable – but if you contemplate travelling when the omens look ill, be sure to follow Rule 2.

Before I leave travel and transport, just a word about tourism, which can be very much associated with and reliant upon differing types of weather.

Most of us tend to 'chase the sun' when it comes to weekends away or longer holidays, so the Mediterranean-type climates of Spain, Greece, California and Florida are appealing. Also popular are the snowfields of the Alps, Rockies and other freezer zones, which offer white walkers the opportunity to express themselves at certain times of the year. Of course, there are many climates in-between, and in excess of those two, worthy of consideration for many reasons beyond weather.

It would be fair to say that the 'A List' destinations of many a holidaymaker almost entirely depend upon the weather, which can go pear-shaped if the worm turns and adverse weather ensues. Alas, that can ruin much-needed getaways and local economies alike. I guess it doesn't happen that often, at least not for long periods, but climate change is arguably changing the face of tourism for good and bad. Recent wildfires and unbearable heat waves are perhaps making us think differently, and surely we're only as good as our last holiday, right?

Climate-related trials and tribulations notwithstanding, I might suggest to tourism professionals that they cherish whatever weather occupies their sweet spot because, without the climate you've been dealt, you probably wouldn't have the attractions currently in place.

And if that isn't good enough for you, when the more helpful weather appears on the horizon, be sharp and shout it out loud and clear. That will surely get the tourists flocking.

Meanwhile, for us tourists and holidaymakers, I point you to Rule 1, because if you are able to be agile, flexible and can change your plans on the turn of the wind, you're acting pretty much like the weather does ... and that can be very helpful!

CHAPTER 15

AFTER THE STORM:
STORM:
INSURANCE AND
LOSS ADJUSTING

The tagline for this chapter could be 'Picking Up the Pieces,' because that's the service provided to us by insurers and loss adjusters, who in large-part can be dependent upon the fear of, or the actuality of weather-related events for their livelihoods.

At this point it's worth noting that I've had more than 30 years' experience working alongside these industries. For the most part, my involvement has been one of providing professional verification in less-definitive weather-related cases, given that major storms, floods and freezes tend to look be entirely self-evident from a verification perspective.

Of course, with every major weather event there are those few who jump onto any passing insurance claim wagon, even if their own damage may have occurred at another time and for different reasons.

Indeed, I've had insured individuals contact the office asking for the date of a storm, as they'd penned a wrong date in their claim form, and the claim consultant hadn't bothered checking other days, or they were simply trying it on. It got so bad at one point that I used to joke, "If anybody is in need of a storm for an insurance claim, just give me a call and I'll find you one!"

The turnover of claims-related staff in the insurance and loss-adjusting world is relatively high, with training on how to handle weather-related claims arguably pretty minimal. The problem with that is that some bona fide claims are mishandled beyond the point of mere frustration, and a few illegitimate claims – made by savvy amateurs or professional con artists – do sneak through.

Akin to weather forecasting, verifying weather-related claims is not an exact science, but in my experience the process could be carried out far more accurately and with a little more surety. I've conducted many seminars on the subject, and audiences have always been anxious to learn about the nuances of lightning strikes, ice damage and wind-related claims.

The science and the art of separating the wheat from the chaff goes all the way back to my navy days, observing the weather's actions for the captain and the aircrew. It was fascinating then, and it still is, just with a different audience and different requirements.

Of course, with climate change rearing its head, the insurance and loss-adjusting industries face huge challenges, with the former likely most prone to financial disaster if climate disasters continue their relentlessly upward financial curve. The test for the loss adjusters is also likely to be a financial one – after all, there is a firm umbilical cord between the two.

But the other challenge could very easily be one of manpower shortages and an inability to meet the many tests that major events and/or climate change may deliver.

On the other side of the coin, of course, both parties could financially benefit in the future, because one step ahead of reality is fear. And yes, fear drives the desire for protection, with financial protection (insurance) likely to be heading the safeguarding queue, at least until weather-impact reality actually strikes.

But even before we consider which comes first in this *chicken or egg* proposition, let's consider the value of the insurance sector becoming a little more proactive than it generally is at present. I advocate a much closer relationship between the insured and the insurers or loss adjusters, well before the shit hits the fan.

Let's face it, we all get a load of useless drivel targeted at us via social media and the like, but here's an opportunity to use the same channels to provide genuinely useful client advice ahead of any impending negative weather scenario. More often than not, all scenarios can be better negotiated with appropriate and timely advice. Call it a comforting arm over a cool shoulder.

Moreover, thinking longer term – whether seasonally or as things continue to unravel with climate change – ongoing communications can be maintained, ensuring that customers become accustomed to how to deal with perils that might have resulted in claims or tragedies.

Insurers could go further into other areas of life and lifestyle, as some mega-companies are doing, but for now let's keep it simple and edge into the future with a little more positivity than perhaps we currently have. And if you happen to be an insurer or loss adjuster, have a gander at the penultimate chapter, which focuses on some things that can help avert or mitigate weather-related disasters.

CHAPTER 16

EVERY CLOUD HAS A LEGAL LINING: WEATHER AND THE LAW

This one comes out of left field, but it's every bit as legitimate as the weather-influenced subjects I have covered so far. You see, every so often weather works its way into some surprisingly strange, sometimes fascinating and occasionally very dark nooks and crannies. This is definitely one of them.

You might think my involvement in legal casework and court cases has everything to do with the previous chapter, concerning insurance-related disputes over slates blowing off roofs during high winds, or somebody allegedly slipping on ice and suing the property owners. That covers a lot of it, but I can add murder, manslaughter, rape, indecent exposure, gross negligence and theft to the list!

For obvious reasons, I won't go into explicit detail on any specific case I've been involved with. Frankly, some of the matters on which I have been asked to impart my knowledge and expertise have been upsetting, and occasionally downright gruesome. Suffice it to say that the weather's impact goes far and wide, and when it comes to murder, simply think through the following: dead bodies, decomposition, location, timing, weather profile and alibis.

The manslaughter cases I've been involved with all tend to follow a similar script, with the accused arguably failing to take adequate precautionary measures in order not to endanger life during various types of hostile weather. A classic example deals with not properly clearing one's vehicle window screen of condensation or ice, and then causing an accident due to restricted vision. The same could be said of the all-too-common practice of travelling too fast during adverse weather, being blinded by a low sun and failing to slow or stop, or in fact moving onward with no idea of what's ahead.

The crux of the matter here is that it is all too easy to slip into a false sense of security and only pay lip service to any type of inhospitable weather that could create problems, for ourselves and those innocents caught in the wrong place at the wrong time.

Temperature and humidity featured prominently in most of the handful of sex-crime cases where I've been called upon to verify weather conditions. There wasn't so much a behavioural link in these cases (though that can be part of the equation), but questions regarding the alleged state of undress.

In this area, and many others in the criminal justice system, I firmly believe that extremities of weather result in peaks and troughs in the incidence of certain crimes and misdemeanors. For example, have you ever wondered why riots don't tend to happen in cold, rainy, miserable weather? And my guess (which is all it is) is that burglaries peak on hot, sunny days, due to open door and window invitations, and taper off when there's snow on the ground, for fear of leaving telltale footprints. But there are always exceptions to the rule, and in the case of that latter situation there are stories of police following such tracks all the way back the culprit's den!

I'll go further, in the hope of opening up a worthwhile line of enquiry. If authorities were to map crimes against weather elements, particularly during extreme events, I'm convinced they'd find a synergy between certain types of weather and certain crimes, as is the case in other areas of life, death and everything in between. Once a correlation is drawn – and it doesn't even have to be that pinpoint-accurate – it should then be possible to predict peaks and troughs of certain crimes, allowing for targeted prevention campaigns and manpower allocation.

Does this sound questionable, or perhaps completely out of the ballpark? Well, if you happen to be involved in law enforcement intelligence, I challenge you to pick up the gauntlet and discover the synergies for yourself. Perhaps you could start with road rage incidents. (Clue: think heat and humidity.)

Now, I'd like to take you to court. Don't be alarmed, I simply mean to offer you a taste of my experiences as an expert witness – me as an amalgam of Inspector Clouseau, Columbo and Miss Marple.

Before entering court I will have completed a site survey, as any of those detectives would have done, searching in my case for meteorological clues, the lay of the land, the local topography, artificial heat sources, obstructions or indeed anything that would potentially sway the weather case this way or that. On occasion that has meant being down on my hands and knees, scouring the ground for clues.

I ended up doing just that in court one day, attempting to explain how black ice isn't really black, and that it might only be discovered by touch as opposed to sight.

So, we're now in court, and far from being daunted by the judge, the jury or the somber proceedings, I actually find it all a challenge and a pleasure. Not to in any way detract from the gravity of a case, the individuals involved or the status of the institution, the courtroom can often be a serious form of theatre. The stage is set, carefully prepared scripts are followed, and the players play their part.

In the end, the judge and jury come to their respective conclusions about what they've heard or seen, and the curtain falls. It is all undeniably dramatic; some may cheer and others will shed a tear.

For many years, it's been my task and my privilege to assist where I have been able to, often providing a ray of light where there was previously considerable mist or fog.

CHAPTER 17

THE HEAT IS ON (OR OFF):
THE ENERGY
SECTOR

For thousands of years, simple open fires provided for our basic energy needs. Up until not so long ago, say the last couple hundred years, very little had changed.

And then ... well, you know the story. The Industrial Revolution. The discovery, processing and use of long-buried coal, oil and gas. Nuclear, hydrogen, solar, wind, geothermal, tidal, hydroelectric, wave and biomass energy. My, haven't we come a long way!

For good or ill, the energy source doesn't really matter – the point here is that the human body functions best at or around 37 degrees Celsius (98.6 Fahrenheit). That inner body temperature is what we strive to maintain, both consciously and unconsciously ... but therein lies a problem. Planet Earth's relationship with the Sun (our primary heat source) varies day by day, season by season, year to year, and from one millennium to the next. And so, we face the perpetual challenge of maintaining our optimum body temperature in order to survive and prosper.

'Survival' may sound a little dramatic, but ask any homeless person, or indeed any inhabitant of polar or desert regions, about the temperature-survival dynamic. They'll have some very definite thoughts on it all.

For most of us, the turn of a dial or flip of a switch gives us what we require: comfort, in the form of extra heat or extra cooling. And, as we all know, that costs money, sometimes a considerable and begrudging outlay. The greater the extremes, and the longer those extremes last, the greater the stress on our bank balance and indeed our wellbeing. Heatwaves and freezing plunges may ensure the financial wellbeing of energy suppliers, but, for most consumers, if the dial is turned it can only lead to fearsome bills dropping through our letter boxes in the weeks ahead.

The basic temperature isn't the only factor in the battle for comfort and survival. Wind speed and direction, the degree of humidity in the air, levels of sunshine and various types of precipitation all play a part. Heat, windchill and comfort indexes take most of those elements into account, reflecting how you might feel at a given point in time, and I'm a big advocate of such indexes when it comes to health and safety.

Of course, there are regions where the ambient mixture of the elements is as damn near perfection as the human body could wish for. In those special places, heating or cooling requirements are considerably minimized, and energy bills will generally follow the same path.

So, where exactly are these 'pleasure zones'?

Well, the tendency is for them to have a semi-tropical or Mediterranean climate, and to usually be coastal or on the lower levels of mountains, or perhaps on the edge of lakes. The consensus appears to offer up Costa Rica as one of those places. Other idyllic spots include Ecuador, Greece, Cyprus, southern Portugal, southern South Africa, northern New Zealand, Bolivia and central Argentina. Others that fit the bill normally offer a good dose of good health to go with lower energy bills.

But the world is changing. What's currently equitable may no longer be in the years to come, and what currently isn't so great may well fall into line. For now, though, our daily requirement for energy – particularly heating and cooling energy – will persist. And so, I offer these simple tips to help keep wearing your '37 degrees' badge with confidence and avoid unnecessarily high power bills.

- **Apparel: your first line of defence.** Always clothe yourself appropriately for the conditions, which can mean taking clothing off as well as putting it on ... and remembering that your head produces the largest outflow of body heat.

- **Feeling cold or hot, always hydrate yourself.** Health practitioners recommend around 2-3 litres of water per day for adults. Don't allow dehydration to compromise your ability to think straight.

- **Consume food and beverages fit for the prevailing weather.** But, also take in stuff that you feel comforted by, excluding alcohol, as any short-term gain there will tend to make for longer-term pain. For those who are familiar with this thermogenic sweetie, a Fisherman's Friend lozenge really can be your friend when the cold bites deep! Also, if you know the big freeze or the sweltering heatwave is on the way, get in the queue early for your vitals, because that queue will only get longer and the shelves will only get emptier.

- **Endeavour to keep your heating/cooling systems well maintained and running at a constant temperature**. Continually turning the switch on and off, or making huge sweeps across the temperature range, is proven to heighten your bill.

- **If cold is the enemy, try to stay active**. Movement creates body heat. If heat is the problem, slow down or even stop and rest.

- **In the cold, if your home is draughty, then stuff any holes, cracks and chasms with whatever you can**. It may look ugly, but it's more important to stay warm than it is for your place to win the best-kept pad award. However weak, allow any sunshine to flow through the windows and feel the difference.

- **In the heat, unblock the same holes, cracks and chasms, allowing your home to breath and win the best-kept pad award**. Natural air movement is a coolant. Prevent direct sunshine from entering any of your rooms; if you don't, your 30 degrees Celsius will be more like 50.

- **In the heat, sleep at the lowest level you can.** Hot air rises and cooler air can be found on or even under the ground floor. In the cold, do the opposite (but please stay off the roof!).

- **If you ever need it, know whom to turn to for help and advice when in any difficultly, even if it's your energy supplier.** Doctors, nurses, local authorities and even your friendly meteorologist should be able to offer you some useful information.

- **Educate yourself.** I haven't got all the answers, and your body and your home are your own. Know what to do and when to do it, and you'll one day warmly (or even coolly) thank yourself for taking the time to do so. More on the merits of useful education in the pages ahead.

CHAPTER 18

READY, AIM, FIRE!: WARS AND BATTLES

Weather will seldom find a place with such gravity, and grave consequence, as the field of battle. I should know, as I was that sailor!

Back in the days of The Falklands War, I was a young pretender, holed up in an underground bunker in north-west London, deciphering weather codes and plotting weather charts to enable British forces to forward plan and negotiate whatever stood in front of them. The weather can be hostile in that part of the South Atlantic – debilitating and obstructive, with hurricane-force winds, poor visibility, freezing temperatures, icebergs, snow and hard rains. They can all play a part in literally making or breaking a mission, a battle or indeed an entire war.

The good news was that the importance of sound weather information was recognized and appreciated, so even at a relatively young age I felt I was respected for my knowledge and usefulness when I finally made it down to the war zone, a couple of weeks after the Argentinians had surrendered.

My job was to brief the captain of my fleet auxiliary ship and the attendant aircrew on the meteorological hazards, which meant hour upon hour, day after day, gazing at the sky and the sea, measuring waves and looking out for any iceberg. But it didn't end there.

You see, there's such a thing as 'ballistic meteorology,' which entails calculating the trajectory of any missile or shell that's fired, taking into account wind, air pressure, temperature and humidity. This was important, because the weather could cause a projectile to go off course and miss the target. So, the elements had to be factored in before any trigger was pulled. It was good that I was on top of all that, since my second part-time job was to man an anti-aircraft gun, and I didn't fancy shooting myself with a six-inch shell that had turned about-face thanks to a fierce wind I hadn't factored in!

That's me and my time frolicking with the weather in the South Atlantic, something I feel fortunate to have done, given the combined might and majesty of The Falklands, South Georgia and the Southern Ocean.

Throughout history, however, fortune and favour may well have been in short supply for the many when faced with the 'wrong weather' in the midst of battle; weather, and the understanding of it, are of utmost importance relative to military strategy and tactics. Get it wrong and it's like turning up for the battle of the bazookas with a pea-shooter ... and there are many commanders, field marshals, captains, admirals and cooks who got it wrong and got burned. (Cooks? Well, if you're supposed to be hidden away from the enemy but when boiling the rat broth the wind catches a hold, then you won't be hidden for very long!)

I digress, but sometimes the little things in weather and war can turn out to be quite big things, if conditions aren't taken into consideration. That can be weather of the moment, short-term weather or longer-term seasonal weather – they all count, for and against, so let the best military meteorologist win. That's more the case in modern times than in centuries gone by, when weather was something of a waiting game, or a complete guessing game, and sometimes ignored completely. As history will reflect, that was nearly always to the detriment of the ignorant.

So, with the knowledge that weather can be super important during conflicts, let's have a little quiz.

Put this book down for a moment, and no peeking. Cast your mind back across history and list as many battles or wars as you can think of that have been won, lost or heavily influenced by weather or climate. Any more than ten (and there are many more), and you certainly know your stuff. It goes to show how weather and climate have shaped our lives, which could be very different had that wind been blowing from the other direction!

So, here's my little list. It may or may not coincide with yours, but they all count ... as much as the weather did then, and will no doubt count again in the future.

- The Battle of Salamis, 480 BC. Weakened by a previous sea storm, the Persian fleet was scuttled by a clever and meteorologically astute Athenian statesman, who used his knowledge of local onshore and offshore winds and their timing to give the smaller and more agile Greek fleet a critical advantage. The result: a notable victory over King Xerxes' forces.

- Mongols fail to invade Japan, 13th century. Two intense monsoon storms defeated Kublai Khan's Mongol army on their way to Japan. Shinto priests believed the stormy winds to be a divine blessing and named them 'Kamikaze.'

- The decimation of the Spanish Armada, 1588. An Atlantic Storm favoured the British. It's sometimes referred to by historians as a 'Protestant Wind.'

- Washington's retreat at the Battle of Brooklyn, 1776. Heavy rains and fog that enveloped New York enabled his 12,000 or so men to escape from the British, and the rest is history.

- The catalyst for the French Revolution, 1780. Prolonged drought, hailstorms, floods and bitter cold made for famine, desperation and the subsequent uprising.

- Napoleon's aborted invasion of Russia, 1812. It all came down to miscalculation of the bitter Russian winter.

- The Winter War, 1939-1940. This conflict between Finland and the Soviet Union, and in particular the Battle of Suomussalmi, saw thousands of ill-clothed Soviet soldiers perish as temperatures plunged below minus-40 degrees Celsius (minus-45 Fahrenheit).

- Hitler's failure to learn from Napoleon, 1941–42. Another bitter Soviet winter and another invader's fatal miscalculation.

- Battle of the Bulge, December 1944. The Germans took advantage of persistently low, grey cloud cover, which grounded the superior US air forces, effectively prolonging by several days what turned out to be the Americans' largest loss of life in any World War II battle.

- Atomic bombing of Nagasaki, 1945. The city of Kokura was the intended target, but heavy cloud cover there meant the pilots opted for the designated alternate target – Nagasaki – where it was partly cloudy.

- Finally, this isn't an individual event, but let's remember the literally millions of civilian and military men, women and children throughout history for whom weather impact meant grief, injury or death. Hostile weather seldom takes prisoners, and has been every bit as deadly as a sword, a bullet or a bomb. To the dead and injured due to weather during warfare, this one is in your honour.

If you are ever unfortunate enough to find yourself in the midst of a war, it will almost certainly be of benefit to take weather into consideration.

EDUCATION! EDUCATION! EDUCATION!:
SCHOOL AND BEYOND

As I wrote in the preface:

> *Weather, or more specifically weather impact, is arguably the most fundamental external factor for every living thing on this fantastically blessed planet of ours. Yet, and for the human contingent only, this all-consuming phenomenon is more often than not taken for granted, ignored or even used as an excuse for failure.*

Well, even if you wish to debate my claim, surely you'll agree that there is enough in it to suggest that weather, climate and their immense impacts should play a significant part in the ongoing education of the masses, a little like the subject of health and wellbeing perhaps.

In a way, this book was written with scholarship and teaching in mind, not to ask any grandmother, any child or anyone in-between to suck eggs. Consider it a primer on matters that effect every single person on this wonderfully colourful planet of ours, and a call for readers to act upon at least a paragraph or two.

In writing this book I have learned things I did not know, things I had forgotten, and things that are of immense importance. If I can still learn after decades of weather-orientated trials and tribulations, then so can everyone else. Indeed, 'You're never too old to learn.' And there are those in positions of power and influence who need to learn, because they know nothing ... or at least they act like they do.

In the mid-1970s, meteorological scholarship consisted of the minimal understanding of basic synoptic situations, such as highs and lows, warm and cold fronts, the seasons, and various climates of the world.

Interesting? Well, possibly. Useful? Yes, if you wished to become a meteorologist, a sailor, a climber or a traveller of some kind. Otherwise, it was just a load of lines and colours on maps with little practical usefulness. For some, I guess it was about as useful as me trying to think of the future use of logarithms (not useful at all).

Of course, both have a place for the few, but for me it all starts and stops when one can find an affinity and a purpose in what is being taught.

At 16 years old, the affinity I certainly had, but the purpose hadn't yet dawned on me. As discussed earlier, I quickly found the purpose, and over the years expanded it to the stretching point, culminating in what you are now reading.

Somewhere in the middle there, I had cause to visit the high school one of my sons was about to enter. The geography classroom was an obvious stopping-off point for me, but to my astonishment I discovered that the small element of meteorology in the geography curriculum was the exact same as when I was a teenager-in-waiting.

What about evolution and progression, I thought? What about climate change, which was at the time beginning to gain traction? What about the politics, those who cared versus those that cared less, the deniers versus the activists? What about the overriding importance of weather and climate's impact on the world of business, and indeed life itself? I realized that schools (at least most British ones) were stuck in a conservative wasteland of rote learning.

There was no evolution, never mind revolution. No stretching beyond the confines of those warm and cold fronts. There was no enterprise, no excitement, and very little understanding of what could be found under a cold stone if it were to be lifted to allow the sunshine in.

Now, I'm not so naïve as to miss that things are not the same the world over, nor for that matter amongst various UK learning establishments. I'm also of the view that at long last things are on the move – more on the warmer climate-change front than on the cooler weather-impact front, but change is happening and it's better late than never.

So, a big 'well done and thank you' to those fleet-footed, imaginative teachers and those brave aspiring students who've seen the light, grasped the nettle and put climate and weather awareness into a higher gear.

A woeful lack of education is partly to blame for the voids and troubles we find ourselves in today, and my foremost challenge in this hugely important area is to help change that. It's imperative that we engage schools, colleges, universities, companies and a rainbow of organizations in understanding the *real* value and importance of weather and climate impact, and prompt them to act upon it.

Before I leave this beautiful but slowly decaying Earth, I am hopeful that kings, queens, presidents, prime ministers, company directors, teachers, mountain climbers, footballers, hairdressers, train drivers, nurses, waiters, cooks, the homeless – indeed, everyone – embrace this all-consuming subject for all it is worth.

I think, I hope and I believe we are at the start of that.

CHAPTER 20

BE WARNED, BE SAFE!: BEST PROTECTION POLICIES

I could not write a book about weather impact without exploring and offering my considered advice on those rare occurrences that are best avoided, where appropriate protection policies can help save lives and limbs.

On the turn of a sixpence the weather can be a beast not to be argued with: fearsome, dreadful, overwhelming and powerful beyond belief. At such times, we can be nothing more than mere ants on a wobbly plank, as Mother Nature chooses to show us her angriest of faces.

In this, the penultimate chapter, I will take you through those sudden, precarious moments that you or someone you know may one day have to contend with. If I can help a single person find protection in a dire situation, I will have succeeded in my aim. The rest is for your back pocket.

In a previous chapter I covered what you might do for comfort, health and safety in times of excessive heat and excessive cold. Particularly with extreme cold, the fatality figures are huge, year in and year out, even in the most developed countries. As I explained in the chapter on health and wellbeing, the knock-on impacts of heatwaves and freezes go far deeper than people simply dying of heatstroke and hyperthermia. Millions suffer miserable deaths, in various ways, as a result of exposure to heat and cold, and many of these deaths are preventable.

So, please spread the word that there are measures one can take to save lives at these times, and some of them are quite simple. If your city, town or village has experienced such fatalities, then the next time you know the thermometer is about to go crazy in either direction, you may be able to save a life by offering your own advice to someone in need.

Here are some suggestions:

Floods: Floods are the leading cause of global weather-related fatalities, and more often than not they're connected to major storms.

This isn't a new phenomenon, created by rising sea levels or other human-influenced disruption. Deaths due to floods – whether directly (drowning or fatal injury) or indirectly (famine/disease) – were far more prevalent in times past.

The worst case appears to have been the 1931 China floods, in which up to 4 million people perished, but there are plenty of other instances of many thousand, or even a million-plus, flood-related fatalities. As recently as 1975, again in China, Typhoon Nina causing the collapse of the Banqiao Dam, which instantly killed more than 80,000 people. Another 50,000 or so succumbed in the aftermath.

Modern-day warning systems, and a deeper knowledge of flood perils and the risk areas, have arguably helped minimize flood impacts over the past half-century. However, global warming and the rise of sea and river levels, coupled with greater-intensity rainfall and the ongoing urbanization of flood plains, could easily take us back a century or two in terms of populations at risk.

What to do, then, if flooding is a peril to be avoided? It sounds pretty obvious, but the best policy is to not live in a high flood-risk zone, be it a river valley or near the sea. Buying a home on a low-lying peninsula jutting out into an ocean that from time to time howls and screams would not be the most sensible move.

Even if you're spending a weekend away, or on holiday in a known flood-prone location, always be aware of what surrounds you and your nearest escape routes, particularly in times of heavy rainfall. Keeping one eye on the local weather forecast might also be advisable – and no, not just on your smart phone. Pay attention to a local radio or TV channel that will be in the know and reporting from the centre of events.

In countries such as Thailand, Vietnam and Laos, villagers in the path of seasonal monsoons often build their houses on stilts. I'm not suggesting that's a solution for everyone, everywhere, but it does show that height counts. So, aim high and stay high when flood peril threatens. If you live in a two-storey building, the second floor will almost always be preferable to the first ... and continue on to the loft or attic space if there is one.

Within those elevated locations, you'd do well to have stored away high-visibility waterproof clothing, emergency food and water (yes, water during a flood!), a working mobile phone (no need for a fancy one), a torch, a whistle, flares, a first aid kit, blankets and a battery-powered radio, in order to listen in on what's happening. As possible, lay in lifejackets, floats and a small dingy, in the event that worse comes to worse.

And remember, if floodwaters have risen to any depth, and your feet are submerged, avoid touching live electrical outputs. Water is a fantastic conductor of electrical currents, and the charge will happily pass through you on its way to the point of least resistance. If your residence has been damaged or compromised, the water itself may be charged, so if you haven't already done so pre-flood, turn the mains switch off.

If you're unsure of the situation, gently test the water by touching the surface with the back of your hand (not the palm or fingers, as that may prove fatal). If electrified, you should feel a small tingle, and you'll know your route is not through the water but over it or around it.

Lightning: This may shock you, but lightning is some six times hotter than the surface of the sun. Each year, as many as 6,000 people worldwide are killed by lightning strikes, with hundreds of thousands more physically injured or traumatized.

Most lighting incidents occur in tropical locations, in developing nations, where thunderstorms are most numerous and most violent, while knowledge of what to do and not do during a thunderstorm is arguably at a minimum.

Agricultural and forest workers are the most at risk, largely because they work in exposed locations where safety is often compromised. Other high-risk groups tend to be in and around susceptible vocations or pastimes, such as fishing, boating or playing field sports such as football and golf. Meanwhile, instances of lightning-related fatalities among domesticated and wild animals far surpass those reported among humans.

The physics of lightning is a complex affair, to say the least, but be aware that lightning is attracted to you, just as you are attracted to it (even though you might not know it or desire it).

What that means is that thunderstorm clouds at their base are generally negatively charged, while you and the stuff around you (trees, blades of grass, posts, fences, chimneys, aerials and that guy next to you) are all positively charged. One charge is always seeking the opposite charge, top to bottom, or bottom to top, in order to produce an electrical current – that is, a pathway, where an electrical discharge can take place.

Think of it as a wavy strand leaving the top of your head and reaching upward, toward the bottom of a thundercloud, where another wavy strand is stretching downward, to meet the strand from your head or nearby objects. If your strand happens to win the 'race,' then expect fireworks – very rapid, explosive and nasty fireworks.

There is another, even more powerful type of lightning strike. It occurs when positive charges at the top of a thundercloud make a direct connection with negative charges at or under ground level. This phenomenon only accounts for around 5% of all lightning, but when it happens, it's with explosive ferocity, and you really don't want to be in its way!

If you do get caught in the wrong place at the wrong time, all is not necessarily lost.

On most occasions you can spot danger on the horizon well before it moves in on you. Keep your eye out for tall, anvil-shaped clouds stretching upward like burgeoning cauliflowers. Next, check the wind direction and ask yourself whether those cauliflower heads are making their way to your plate. If you think they may be, don't waste a moment moving to safety, as lightning can strike from up to ten miles away. Despite that distance, it can take mere milliseconds for your comfort zone to become a lot less comfortable.

If you're in the danger zone, watch for distinct bodily feelings that can portend a lightning strike, like prickly or sweaty/tingly sensations, hair standing on end, a metallic taste in the mouth, a chlorine-like smell in the air, a feeling of being off-balance or dizzy, and sounds of cracking or buzzing. If any of these occur, you're probably in imminent danger. If all of them occur at once, don't forget to wave a very quick goodbye!

If you are stuck, lessen the impact by crouching down, with your feet together, in a tight ball. Don't lie flat; don't stand in a puddle or jump into a pond, lake or the sea; don't hang around under a tall object such as a tree, goal post or a boat mast.

The inside of a vehicle offers some protection, but it's not foolproof, and avoid touching any metal parts that will conduct a lightning strike to the ground. Contrary to popular belief, rubber tyres make no difference, just as rubber-soled shoes or Wellington boots don't.

If you happen to be indoors during a violent lightning event, stay away from the plumbing (showers, baths and sinks), electrical systems (TVs, computers, hairdryers), concrete floors and walls, and landline phones. All of these conduct electricity, and you don't want join the circuit.

Tornadoes: They may appear to be a distinctly American scourge, but these terrible beasts of the weather world occur virtually everywhere. They strike Russia and India, the UK and other parts of Europe, as well as South America and Australia. But yes, the biggest twisters consistently hit the infamously-named 'Tornado Alley' that stretches across the southern and central US.

When tornado warnings are sounded, the best plan of action is to get on your horse and ride like the wind. But tornadoes can spawn very quickly, often without warning, and reach full force within a matter of minutes. They're unpredictable and awesome in their power, with central winds in a worse-case Fujita scale 'Force 5' whirlwind blowing up to 300 mph. That's powerful enough to drive nails deep into wood and pick big, mature trees up as if they were matchsticks.

So, what to do if a tornado is bearing down on you? Your first move should be to aim low. A cellar or basement often offers the best protection within a typical abode. Failing that, head for the central part of the house, and the smaller the space, the better – closets with four walls are a good example. For sure, keep away from windows and forget roof spaces; acute danger lurks in and around both.

If you have time, try to turn off the electricity and gas at the mains.

Another objective is to cover oneself in 'armour.' Jump into a fixed bathtub, as they tend to be pretty robust, and layer on as much bodily protection as possible, using blankets, cushions, pillows and extra layers of bulky clothing. Utilize anything that can deflect flying objects ... or that can cushion yourself if you happen to become the flying object. If you have cycle or sports helmets and protective padding, wear them. It doesn't matter how ridiculous you may look, this is a matter of survival.

You might also consider tying yourself and others to anything that seems unmovable, since being flung around like a rag doll won't help your cause. By the way, if you don't use the bathtub for shelter, fill it with water, as this may prove to be a valuable source of clean water after the event.

If you're caught out in the open, once again the objective should be to aim low. Climb into a ditch or a hole and lay flat, covering your head. Vehicles and underpasses are a no-go; they won't offer any protection as a funnel cloud descends.

Finally, in the aftermath, when it all settles down again, emerge with caution and tread carefully. There are bound to be hazards aplenty, including hanging debris, exposed nails, razor-sharp metal and glass, live electrical wires and ruptured gas mains, not to mention confused, injured, altogether unpredictable animals.

Hurricanes/Typhoons: The one positive thing concerning these monsters of the oceans is that, nowadays, population centres invariably receive ample warning. Technology affords us a relatively accurate view of their status, track and potential impact timing. But that's where the good news ends.

During hurricane or typhoon activity – and the same can be said of major, but less powerful, storm types – most fatalities occur because of drowning during sea or river inundation, or simply due to overpowering volumes of rainwater. In these situations it's necessary to go back a few pages and revisit what to do during flooding. If high winds are the main concern, then the rules for protection from tornadoes apply.

In all such emergencies, it is important to follow your local authorities' or national government's advice, although not necessarily verbatim, as every situation demands a degree of thinking on one's feet. However, evacuation orders should never be ignored, and the experts' advice has been tested and proven to save lives.

Avalanches: This is the age-old bane of mountain climbers, skiers and others who live in or frequent snowy mountainous areas. The first rule here is to take the advice of officials who oversee the mountain range. If they're warning of an avalanche risk (even a small one), then definitely buy into what they are selling.

Perhaps not surprisingly, the vast majority of avalanches occur in the winter, with some overlap into late autumn and early spring, when snowfalls can pile up one on top of another. Warning signs include acute changes in the weather, such as heavy snowfalls followed by much warmer temperatures. If you see other avalanches at a distance, or even minor snow slides around you, you can assume there's a heightened risk.

While walking, you may notice cracks appearing in the snow, or your footsteps might sound hollow, or they may even give a thumping sound, all of which indicate potential instability. During or just after a period of high winds, drifts of snow or strangely shaped heaps or clusters tend to be unstable, and prone to snapping off and sliding away under the force of gravity.

Most avalanches are triggered by natural causes – for example, during snowstorms – simply due to uneven, heavy loads piling on top of previously compressed snow slabs. Other natural triggers include melting snow on sunny days, undermining rain, rockslides or icefalls, lightning strikes and earth tremors. Unnatural triggers – those attributable to humans and local animal life – can also disturb the peace in one way or another, to equally catastrophic effect.

As with any form of weather adversity, surviving an avalanche requires appropriate 'just-in-case' planning, and then certain definitive actions.

The planning starts with wearing appropriate, highly visible clothing to cope with the elements and be seen from a distance. It also means carrying high-calorie food to last for at least 24 hours, water, a torch, a whistle and a lightweight sleeping bag or one of those silver space blankets. Also consider packing a foldaway spade and an avalanche transceiver, which can lead rescuers to your pinging signal if you end up buried.

However, before you plump for the 'buried alive' option, think about how you might act if an avalanche was heading toward you.

The first trick is to try to move away from the centre of the onslaught – the sides of an avalanche are less powerful. If the snow collapses beneath you, jump upslope and keep jumping until you land on firmer snow. If that didn't work, quickly ditch any unnecessary heavier items, such as the camera, tent, spare boots, cans of beer and anything else that will simply weigh you down and take you further into the snowy depths. If you can, grab onto something solid, such as a stout tree or a rocky outcrop, and try your best to cling on.

OK, so the tree broke and you and the tree are now careering down the mountain. What now? Those who have experienced such situations say to 'swim' as fast as you can with the snow. A front crawl is best, but whatever the stroke, swim for all you're worth to stay on top of the snow flow.

If the doggy paddle didn't work, and you're now buried, you hopefully closed your mouth and gritted your teeth while swimming. That would have helped you avoid immediate asphyxiation, the leading cause of death during avalanches. Don't panic and try to stay calm ... which is probably easier said than done with a ton of snow sitting on your face. If you can move your arms, try to scrape out a hole above your nose and mouth and slowly take a deep breath, filling your lungs. Keep breathing slowly and deliberately, but don't bother shouting or screaming, as nobody will hear you – snow is an excellent absorber of sound.

If you've gotten this far, there is no definitive time limit for survival, although some say up it could be around 15 minutes at that point. Regardless, positivity, hope and good fortune are arguably your best friends during your wait for rescue.

Wildfires: It's not so much the fire that's the weather element, though lightning is one of the prime causes of fast-moving vegetation fires. It's more the wild bit ... namely, winds, and specifically high winds. Wildfires, particularly those of late across California, the Amazon, Mediterranean Europe and parts of Australia, have become something of a hell on earth as global warming leads to prolonged droughts and tinderbox forests and fields.

Wildfires tend to be summer or early autumn events, and autumn blazes have been particularly notorious.

The October 1825 Miramichi fire in the US state of Maine and neighboring New Brunswick, Canada, killed around 150 people and destroyed three million acres of forest, leaving 15,000 homeless. The Peshtigo Fire of October 1871 ravaged 3.7 million acres of Wisconsin and Michigan, killing an estimated 2,000 people. In recent years, wildfires have ravaged huge swathes of Australia, Spain and Portugal.

If there is a commonality between almost all massive wildfires, it is that they tend to occur within or just after hot and bone-dry summers, driven along by strong winds.

Given a changing climate, I can only see this phenomenon going in one direction.

These fires can be every bit as unpredictable as a tornado, but if you get caught in or around one, your home is unlikely to save you. Your best bet is to get out of the danger zone as soon as humanly possible, and to stay alert to your exit options. A motor vehicle does have protective qualities, and can move faster than you can run, so that's an obvious plus in any firestorm. But don't just drive off aimlessly. Strategize your escape, perhaps by first finding a higher observational point to search for a clear route out.

Wildfires move with the wind, and you hardly want to be heading toward the heart of the inferno as you attempt to flee. Having said that, depending on the wind speed, trying to outpace a wildfire can be problematic. If you're on foot, that may be impossible. The trick is to move perpendicular to the fire, outflanking it with the ability to keep a keen eye on its movement.

If there is a choice between going uphill or downhill, head downward. Heat rises, fire rises, smoke rises, and uphill is where it will all naturally want to go. At all costs, avoid deep ravines; once in there a fire can turn into a furnace, as the wind is funneled between the steep sides.

One invaluable tip: if you spy a potential exit route with already-burnt timber or brush, that really is your way out – there is no more fuel there to feed the flames.

If the wildfire has surrounded you, with no obvious way out, what then? If you're near a seashore, lake, pond, river, or even a decent-sized swimming pool, submerging yourself in the water will offer a high degree of protection. That is, if you aren't too close to burning trees or buildings that could fall onto you.

Barring those options, the final resort is to seek shelter in and around the ground. Find a hole free from trees and shrubs, and if you can't find one, dig one. If possible, cover yourself in wet woolen blankets, or soil, or any non-flammable protective covering. Finally, and don't worry about any ants or worms, they will have longed planned their escape route, push your face into the ground, stiffen your upper lip and cross everything!

The chances of you ending up in any of these perilous weather situations is arguably slim, unless you choose to put yourself in harm's way. However, the world *is* changing, and what could once have been considered a relatively safe planet – with weather extremes only occurring where they usually prowled – is no more.

And with that, I urge you to take note, keep this book/ chapter in a handy place, exercise care and stay safe.

CLIMATE CHANGED: BEATEN BY THE DINOSAURS?

And so, we arrive at the final chapter of our journey, aloft on our comfy cloud, sailing through the world of weather impact, and gliding into the reaches of long-term climate change.

I say 'long-term' change, but based on these past few decades it's evident beyond any reasonable doubt that uncertainty is becoming the new weather normal.

Ours is now a world of year-on-year changes and serious weather impacts, with climate-change manifestations of all shapes and colours. Indeed, the tumultuous climate-impact year of 2019 arguably topped the lot (at least at time of publication).

Not long after I formed BWS, back in late 1988, I distinctly recall the profound US Senate testimony of James E. Hansen, a climate scientist who claimed the greenhouse effect had been detected and was already changing our climate. He wasn't the first person to warn that this posed a future threat to the world, and he certainly won't be the last, but it was a pivotal moment. The message reached a worldwide audience, some of whom already feared for the future, amid gradually rising sea levels.

Hansen's words certainly struck a chord with me. Instinctively, rather than via any scientific evidence, I felt at the time that a genie had been unleashed from the bottle and the world as we know it was on a path to a series of catastrophes and potential oblivion.

Moreover, the scientific evidence, although not entirely conclusive at the time, would over the years become only stronger, with fossil-fuelled mankind implicated as the root cause. I recall writing a piece for a national newspaper about what we might expect in 30 or so years' time. And now ... well, we're here.

Let me say something else for the record: I'm a hypocrite. I was then, I was in the interim, and I remain so now in many of my daily actions. Even if there was only a small chance that our behaviour would cause our world to fail, I largely acted as if I could just go on doing things like I'd always done.

Yet, as a practising meteorologist, with my finger on the pulse and statistics at my fingertips, I'm in a position that carries a tad more responsibility.

That I know what I know makes me a bigger hypocrite than most, and I sincerely apologize for not having picked up the baton earlier. But now is my time, and via my consulting work, social media posts, and hopefully this book, I will do my bit and continue to pick up some of the litter I dropped during my lifetime.

I am on the proverbial road to Damascus, though it will take me the rest of my life to arrive there!

One of the main arguments against man-made climate change is that our climate changes *naturally*, and has done so for millions of years. This current change,

WEATHER OR NOT?

some would argue, is part of a *natural cycle*. The story of the Earth is indeed one in which climate has changed time and again, for the good, for the bad and the ugly. Ice ages, persistent droughts and warm interglacial periods have long made for a heady mixture.

The Earth's relationship with the sun is part of the reason, with gradual, periodic changes in the angle of the Earth to the sun (its *obliquity*). I won't attempt to explain it other than to say that our planet, or different parts of it, receives varying amounts of solar radiation, and that has a direct climate impact. Add sporadic solar flare activity and other solar influences, and we have the reasons why some non-believers in man-made climate change pin it solely on that big ball of fire.

So, if you're looking for a reason why grapes were reportedly grown in the normally temperate northern English city of York some 2,000 years ago, look no further than the obliquity at the time.

Heading further back to when dinosaurs ruled the Earth – a period that lasted for around 250 million years – the world itself was a very different place. The various tectonic plates initially locked together as a single landmass known as Pangaea, which from one millennium to the next experienced diverse climates that supported the broad family of dinosaurs. When the climate gradually changed, most of the dinosaurs adapted. When it changed rapidly, certain species became extinct and others took their place.

Major climate changes occurred during the age of the dinosaurs, and they took their toll, but the granddaddy of them all came just prior to the emergence of 'the terrible lizards.' It wiped out 85% of living species and is known today as the P-T extinction. The exact cause is unknown, but it's believed that climate change was at the heart of it, possibly due to a colossal release of methane (ten times more potent than carbon dioxide as a greenhouse gas) from under the oceans.

We all know that even during a relatively short period of time – a couple of centuries is absolutely nothing on the greater cosmic clock – climate can vary. Except where volcanic eruptions are involved, those variances tend to be in hundreds or tenths of a single degree. Yet, those small changes in air and ocean temperatures yield flowing rivers that were once frozen solid, and once-verdant forests withered into barren deserts.

Those variances have been largely due to natural climate-impact events ... but what has landed upon us in the past 30 years or so is about as natural as a rubber duck.

And yet, despite the mass of evidence, near-100% agreement among climate scientists, most governments now agreeing that climate change has become a real and increasing threat to the world as we know it, climate deniers continue to deny. They still troll the world of social media and walk the corridors of power.

When I first thought about this chapter, I really did think I'd attempt to be balanced and provide oxygen to the counter-arguments of the deniers. Well, in mentioning their insistence that the changes are 'natural,' that's all the leeway I'm prepared to give them. As far as I'm concerned, they can suck on all the methane and carbon dioxide they emit.

Even if, in the long term, they turn out to have been right all along and the scientists prove to be ridiculously wrong (which I'm convinced won't happen), the deniers should at least acknowledge that there's a possibility they might be wrong. Perhaps they could recognize that actions to prevent a rapidly warming world from tipping over the edge may be entirely appropriate.

But no, in my mind it's denial for purely selfish and self-centred reasons, usually wrapped in power, money or both. Sadly, over the past few years, the political complexions of major countries (the US, Brazil, Australia) have gone the way of the climate-change deniers. We see the debate being smothered by 'more important issues,' obfuscation and downright lies.

Well, world, you can't eat money and you can't drink deceit, and the deniers are truly the callous, modern-day dinosaurs. They are precisely what our planet does not need at this pivotal time in mankind's history. Let's hope they go extinct before we all do.

So, here we are then, at a time when the Earth's climates have already dramatically changed, and will change further, in a world full of know-nothings and poisonous nihilists. But there are those who do know, who do care, who fear for all our futures. It's taken a couple of generations for this battle to rage, and the global 'do something now' movement is gathering pace, not from the top down but from the bottom up. It's the young who are standing tall, demonstrating and making their rightfully angry but hopeful voices heard.

Of course, it's not only about the climate. The environment in general is under siege, with plasticization, ocean and soil contamination, noise and light pollution, the wanton (or even accidental) destruction of the Earth's ecologies, and much more. It's all part of the truly awful way in which humans have defecated in our own nest.

We may have reached tipping points as far as plasticization, light and noise pollution, and the ongoing destabilization of ecological systems are concerned ... or we're pretty damn close. Sadly, with the use and disposal of plastics at an all-time high – and the world's population pushing eight billion, from an already-unsustainable six billion at the turn of the 21st century – I cannot offer any viable or morally acceptable solutions.

For example, it would be an immense and noble aim to recycle all the waste plastic in the world, except doing so would take an extraordinary amount of energy and water, which in turn would produce billions of tons of carbon dioxide, adding to global warming. I'd call that a Catch-22 if ever there was one.

Earlier in this book I said you might not like what I have to say about climate change and the direction we're now travelling. Well, despite the aim to limit the global air temperature rise to 1.5 degrees Celsius during this current century, I do not think the human race has a cat in hell's chance of achieving that. Not with a growing global population, developing nations industrializing, couldn't-care-less major governments (even if they say they do care), and the Greenland ice mass and other ice sheets, ice shelves, icebergs and major glaciers all shrinking way.

Climate change is not a theory; it's not even a debate anymore. The climate of this world of ours *has* changed, and humankind is the reason for that change. From this point onward, we are fighting a losing battle, akin to the Titanic *after* it hit that fateful iceberg, and we all know how that ended.

The consequences of this continuing change from the Earth's natural state are many, and likely to be extremely unnerving. Since rapid climate change fosters high levels of unpredictability across the board, I won't bandy around meaningless figures regarding rising sea level rises. I won't try to catalogue the number of island nations and coastal cities that will come under the direct threat of permanent coastal flooding. I won't list the regions that will become drought-ridden and prone to cataclysmic fires. I will not try to name the areas that will see their rainfall double and triple.

And don't take my word for the potential severity. The Intergovernmental Panel on Climate Change (IPCC), which includes more than 1,300 scientists from the US and other countries, recently warned: "Taken as a whole, the range of published evidence indicates that the net damage costs of climate change are likely to be significant and to increase over time."

I recently asked Larry Cosgrove, the respected Chief Meteorologist at WEATHERAmerica – a consultancy serving the trading, energy, transportation, agriculture and insurance industries – for his valued opinion. "Through the past decade," he told me, "many around the world have become aware of the building threat of global warming. The challenge of the next ten years will be to both study the effects of climate change and introduce new technologies which will, in time, reverse the hazards and alterations, in order to make our world a safer and better place."

The first is a stark warning, the second holds out hope, but both are solid enough to warrant ultra-serious attention. The precise details of what will happen from here on in are down to the biggest lottery since the last great extinction.

The consequences I've mentioned are for the most part public knowledge – though not accepted by the modern-day dinosaurs – but I have yet to mention other potential serious fallouts. If you've read this book from cover to cover, you will hopefully be of the opinion that weather and climate are indeed integral to the way we live our lives. That applies to yesterday, today and all our tomorrows, however many tomorrows there actually are.

In the foreseeable future, there's probably no more important issue at stake here than our own safety, health and wellbeing. Yet, a warmer world will almost certainly mean a greater threat from water-borne diseases and those carried by insects and rodents.

Countries or regions that were considered 'safe zones' won't be, placing immense stress on affected populations and health authorities. New diseases akin to the coronavirus are also likely to emerge – maladies that scientists have no immediate cure for. Meanwhile, new and old diseases may well decimate already climatically-stressed global food crops and livestock, resulting in food shortages ... and, in the extreme, starvation and forced mass migration. Similar forced migrations of one size or another may occur due to precious water sources drying up, or unwanted water inundating towns and cities.

Once we find ourselves in a world where mass migration steepens to the point where neighbouring countries can't cope, we're deep into economics, politics and erratic actions, which could easily spiral into civil unrest and even war. And before anybody laughs off my warning, remember that wars have occurred over far less than forced mass displacement.

Are you beginning to get an idea of some of the stresses the world may have to endure when air and ocean temperatures continue their frightening climb?

It's also worth saying that a warmer world will not necessarily be one void of acute cold and protracted severe winters. The near certain displacement of the polar vortexes more often than currently occurs will mean sudden, unpredictable swings from sub-tropical warmth one month to crippling, protracted freezes the next. Those short-sighted individuals who consider global warming a mere distraction (after all, what's a couple of degrees?) may have to think again when the freezer decides to park itself on their doorstep for six long, frigid months.

It all sounds a tad grim, doesn't it? A little like those Armageddon films that appear on our screens from time to time … but it's all very real. Just ask those caught up in the terrible wildfires of 2019 in California and Australia, while their respective heads of state laid low, very low.

So, can we really do anything to literally stem the tide and avoid a Titanic-like disaster?

Well, the first thing we have to consider is the timescale of things, and in that there has to be a big question mark, as we're treading new ground. If and when the tipping point is breached, an acceleration of the various impacts will surely follow. That means we're already chasing our tail, and in order to catch it we must first slow down the acceleration. Since that acceleration is only just under way, we have a long way to travel in the wrong direction before the brakes start to kick in.

But then, there's another scenario to consider. Perhaps we're travelling too fast already, and any brakes we care to apply might be spongy at best and useless at worst. Back to that word 'Armageddon,' I guess!

However, I'm an optimist by nature, and even if Mother Nature is about to take vengeance on our careless, wanton ways, humankind will still endeavour to avert the worst, even if it takes a hundred years or more.

So, here are my top tips for surviving the impacts, making it to the lifeboats and setting course for a bright, new, secure future ... even if it might not be for you in person!

1. **Vote**. At election time, if you have a vote, use it wisely. Put climate change pledges above everything else, because everything else will fall asunder if nothing is done. GDP could also be translated as *Grossly Dumb Practices*, as ever-increasing national GDPs at this moment in time can only mean ever-increasing global warming. If the incumbents have done little or nothing to offset the risks during their time in office, they'll almost certainly do nothing again if re-elected. Find the person or party that genuinely embraces realistic and imaginative climate change policies, and don't be browbeaten by the siren voices of the climate

change-denying machine, generally found on the far right of politics and often snuggled up with the fossil fuel industry. Vote for the deniers, the nihilists or the dullards and the greatest single influence you can have in terms of reshaping the future will go up in smoke. And if nobody standing for election supports your views ... well, if you're able, why not consider running for office yourself?

2. **Join local climate action groups.** Share ideas and take meaningful action. I'm not talking about climbing on top of trains or lying across roads, inconveniencing many of those that may support your cause! Your tasks should be practical on the one hand and persuasive on the other. Beat the deniers at their own game: plan local or regional campaigns that articulately stress the truth about the present and future impacts of climate change, and what might be done.

3. **Go green.** By that I mean plant trees, bushes and other greenery, all of which are carbon dioxide eaters. In the case of trees, it's perhaps better done in a managed way, under the auspices of local groups or authorities. But even inside your home or office, that tiny plant on your desk is a tiny positive. Every little bit helps. As we discovered in the chapter on health and wellbeing, green is a beneficial colour ... but also feel free to explore other colours in your

noble endeavours. (Just less of the *tombstone grey*, perhaps!)

4. **Go green ... again!** Choose a natural energy provider, if at all possible, selecting one that utilizes wind, solar or tidal power. Banish the fossil fuel merchants to the deep hole they extracted their polluting merchandise from.

5. **Eat less meat**. I don't say eat no meat; for many that would be like asking them to pee into the wind on a daily basis. Change for the many is by small steps, and when added up, that eventually amounts to something. Intensive livestock farming accounts for 10–20% of annual greenhouse gas emissions, and over time you can make a significant dent. Pass the sprouts!

6. **Use your legs**. We all depend on trains, planes and automobiles, almost all of which are fossil-fuelled. For small journeys, aim for a day per week (or more if you can) to walk, run, skip or jump to wherever you're going. It'll help make you more fit (a worthwhile bonus) while you gradually reduce unfriendly emissions, as demand for polluting transportation declines. For longer journeys, if there's a choice, take the train as opposed to the plane. Aeroplanes are among the top atmospheric polluters; those white *chemtrails* they etch across the sky contain pollutants as well as crystallised water vapour.

If you intend to buy or rent a car, go electric. You won't be the first, but you might be the last if you keep putting it off.

7. **Be smart in your home**. Talk to your suppliers about energy-saving devices and measures to reduce carbon emissions. Be frugal with your energy use – do you really need the hot water so hot that it's too hot to touch? Could you don a pair of socks if your feet are chilly rather than turning up the heat? If you have south-facing windows, allow the sun to shine in when it's needed and pull the curtains when it's not. Small steps, maybe, but the bonus here is that you'll save money as well as the planet ... and feel pretty good about it.

8. **Utilize the products and services of 'green' companies instead of 'couldn't-care-less' companies**. It may take some effort and research, and sometimes it may cost a little more (at least for now), but if enough people decide to walk the talk, then price reductions should follow.

9. **Don't buy or rent houses on river floodplains or flood-prone coastal strips**. If you do, you're simply asking for it. You're just suckering up to the deceit of those who would choose to build simply for profit, with little concern for your future welfare.

10. **Companies and organizations that have done nothing, start doing something!** It may not make commercial sense, or even common sense right now, to jump aboard the climate-change bandwagon and begin taking steps that will make a difference in the future. Indeed, it's well past the wakey-wakey stage. But for the uninformed, the deniers or the plain lazy, it's not too late to change tack and grasp what might appear to be an inconvenient, but potentially nasty, stinging nettle. The alternative is one where even the most outlandish risks become a reality, and then there will be no businesses, no prospects and no future.

For a brief moment, I'll try to remain optimistic about the future. You see, despite signs that we may be beyond the point of ever getting back to a state of stability and security, there is one possible saving grace: technology.

We definitely cannot control the weather – it controls us. But humankind has the ability to invent, reinvent and find novel ways of overcoming threats to our existence. That doesn't mean building bigger walls, walls that deflect water to someone else's front door, or any of that inane thinking. I'm not brilliant enough to say what technologies might see the light of day and save our bacon, but I didn't foresee the invention of smartphones or artificial intelligence.

It's a mighty challenge, and one that may yet be lost, but there has to be some optimism that technological advances – together with awareness and the will to act – will enable us to reopen the windows of our self-made greenhouse and turn back the climate clock.

And finally ...

If, in the end, I haven't managed to persuade you of the immense magnitude and critical importance of climate and weather in our daily lives – and within the various ecosystems that every living thing on this planet inhabits – then good luck to you. You're going to need as much luck as you can muster.

On the other hand, if I have in any way educated, enthused, entertained or enthralled you, then thank you for being open-minded and sticking with me.

Think about the title of this book: *Weather or Not?* It's a choice; it always has been.

You can ignore what's all around you, every single day – that which guides and affects you, and all life on Earth, from birth to death. Or, you can feel it, understand it, embrace it, use it, share it, love it.

Most of all, you can choose to protect it, for our climate and weather can be our greatest friends... or our end of days.

Let the watch begin!

Smell the earth,
Behold the sky,
Silver raindrops to make you cry.

Hold on tight,
Fall to your knees,
Caress the power of the breeze.

Rub your eyes,
Praise the cloud,
It's a brilliant rainbow to make you proud.

Search for the magic,
Kiss the cold,
Capture a snowflake of purest gold.

Hug the sun,
Absorb its heat,
This one is hard to beat.

Grasp the air,
It's as light as a feather,
You are now a scholar of the weather!